30 Days with Jesus

EXPERIENCING HIS PRESENCE THROUGHOUT
THE OLD AND NEW TESTAMENTS

LYSA TERKEURST

and

DR. JOEL MUDDAMALLE

HarperChristian
Resources

30 Days with Jesus
© 2023 by Lysa TerKeurst and Dr. Joel Muddamalle

Requests for information should be addressed to:
HarperChristian Resources, 3900 Sparks Dr. SE, Grand Rapids, Michigan 49546

ISBN 978-0-310-16108-0 (softcover)
ISBN 978-0-310-16109-7 (ebook)

HarperChristian Resources titles may be purchased in bulk for church, business, fundraising, or ministry use. For information, please e-mail ResourceSpecialist@ChurchSource.com.

First Printing September 2023 / Printed in the United States of America

23 24 25 26 27 LBC 5 4 3 2 1

Although you will find each day's teaching assigned to either Lysa or Joel, both authors contributed to every teaching. The choice of author was to assign the personal story shared.

I was in a season where I'd been doing church for a long time. But I kept having this suspicion that other Christians had a more direct line to God than I had. Things just seemed to work out for them. They kept gratitude journals and shared incredible revelations they'd had in their personal time with God.

I would hear their confidence and silently wonder what was I missing?

I didn't want to say it. I didn't want to feel it. I didn't want to be struggling with it. But the real response in my heart said, "I'm not sure the Lord is really with me."

Sometimes I would feel a rush of assurance when standing in worship or when something big happened and I could declare, "Wow, look what the Lord did!" But most days I just kept quiet and faked like I had the same unwavering spiritual confidence that everyone else had.

All the while, internally, I couldn't shake this nagging thought that if Jesus really cared about me and wanted a relationship with me, why couldn't I see Him, hear Him, and get to know Him? I mean, if a human relationship was this mysterious, I'd assume the person was ghosting me and giving me the not-so-subtle hint to move on.

Then I remembered some relationship advice I'd heard: If you want to improve your connections with friends and family, you need to communicate your desires more clearly.

SO I WROTE IN MY JOURNAL THREE DESIRES I HAD FOR MY RELATIONSHIP WITH JESUS:

1. I want to see You.
2. I want to hear You.
3. I want to know You.

My heart was crying out to see evidence of God's reality in my life. I truly wanted to experience His presence and walk in the assurance that He saw me, heard me, and wanted to know me. So one day I decided to turn that journal list into a prayer I would pray each day. And eventually I added, "I want to follow hard after You every day so before my feet hit the floor, I say 'yes' to You."

After praying that prayer each day, I started looking for God with greater intentionality throughout my day and start living with expectation of this prayer being answered.

It's now been over 20 years since I started praying this prayer. And every part of my life has been positively impacted as I live with expectation of experiencing Him daily.

I can't say that doubt doesn't ever creep back in my mind. There have been some times in the past few years where doubt has shown back up, and I wondered: Jesus, where are You?

During a particularly difficult time, I asked God to help me know with greater assurance, confidence and courage that He was with me. And He did, in such an unexpected way. As I was reading the first two chapters of Genesis, God showed me that Jesus is very much mentioned in the creation story. And I realized that if Jesus was never absent in Scripture from beginning to end, He wasn't absent from my life either.

And that is when I went searching for Jesus throughout the entire Bible, to confirm and reassure me of His presence in unexpected ways in my life today.

Jesus has never been one to hide. And He's certainly not hiding from us now. We just have to know how He presents Himself all throughout Scripture so that we can see how present He is in every aspect of our lives today.

If you've been through some tough realities in your life lately, or if you want to better prepare for seasons of hardship with more comfort, confidence, and courage, then you're in the right place.

AND IF YOU'VE BEEN LONGING FOR:
Greater comfort that Jesus is near . . .
Greater confidence that Jesus cares . . .
Greater courage that you aren't fighting alone . . .

Then, welcome, friend, to this special study about Jesus.

Joel and I thought about you through our writing, and we can't wait to share all we've learned with you, together.

Love,

Lysa TerKeurst
AUTHOR

Dr. Joel Muddamalle
AUTHOR

Shae Hill
MANAGING EDITOR

Glynnis Whitwer
EDITORIAL SUPPORT

As we begin our study of Jesus throughout Scripture, it may be surprising to learn that Jesus didn't first appear in Matthew.

Jesus has been present from the very beginning. John 1:1 declares that Jesus was present in the Genesis 1–2 creation story: *"In the beginning was the Word, and the Word was with God, and the Word was God."* Verse 14 clarifies even further that *"the Word became flesh and dwelt* among us*, and we have seen his glory, glory as of the only Son from the Father, full of grace and truth"* (emphasis added).

Nothing was created without Jesus (John 1:1–14) and everything is perfected by Jesus. We can see Jesus as the one who perfects what humans can only do in part. In the Old Testament, there were three offices of leadership that led the people of God: prophet, priest, and king. However, everyone in the Old Testament who held these offices did so imperfectly. The reality of these imperfections created an even deeper anticipation for the promised Messiah who would eventually hold all three offices, but in complete perfection.

It's the truth of Jesus as the Greater Prophet (Matthew 13:57; Luke 7:16), Priest (Matthew 1:21–23; 1 Timothy 2:5,[1] and King (Matthew 1:1; 9:27; 12:23; 15:22) that gives meaning and understanding to every word, sentence, paragraph and page of the Bible from Genesis to Revelation. **Without the presence of the promised Messiah in the Old Testament, we cannot fully understand or grasp the brilliant truth and glory of Jesus on display in the New Testament.**

Jesus is never absent in God's story, and He's certainly not absent in any part of our story either. Jesus is our guide, our context, and our example. Not just through the Bible but throughout our lives.

In fact, the entire Bible testifies to the promise, presence, protection and proclamation of the peace that Jesus provides. And aren't we most desperate for this kind of assurance when our future seems unclear, our prayers seem to go unanswered, and more unexpected heartbreaks make us want to doubt?

Is Jesus actually there?

Yes, He is.

Does He actually care?

Yes, He does.

OVER THE NEXT THIRTY DAYS WE'LL LOOK FOR AND DISCOVER
JESUS IN SCRIPTURE USING SIX DIFFERENT LENSES. EACH ONE
WILL SHOW US SOMETHING SURPRISING AND ENCOURAGING,
AND CONFIRM GOD'S GOOD PLAN FOR US.

WEEK ONE

Portraits

We see glimpses of Jesus through people in the Bible, as they partially fulfilled what He would later completely fulfill.

WEEK TWO

Prophecies

We see Jesus through the prophecies that tell of His coming in the flesh.

WEEK THREE

Patterns

We see Jesus in alternating patterns in the Bible like famine and rain, or wilderness and promised land that help us connect to the consistent reality of the presence of Jesus.

Provisions

We see Jesus in God's physical, emotional, and spiritual provision for the people of the Old Testament as Jesus is our perfect provision for all our needs.

Protections

We see Jesus through God's protection of His people, as we start to discover the ultimate protection we have in Him.

Presence

We see God's desire to be near His people since creation, and the ultimate invitation to be with Him is in Jesus.

In the beginning, God created
the heavens and the earth.

GENESIS 1:1

The earth was without form and
void, and darkness was over the
face of the deep. And the Spirit of
God was hovering over the face of
the waters.

GENESIS 1:2

And God said, "Let there
be light," and there was light.

GENESIS 1:3

And God saw that the light was
good. And God separated the light
from the darkness.

GENESIS 1:4

God called the light Day, and the
darkness he called Night. And
there was evening and there was
morning, the first day.

GENESIS 1:5

In the beginning was the Word, and the Word
was with God, and the Word was God.

JOHN 1:1

He was in the beginning with God.

JOHN 1:2

All things were made through him,
and without him was not any thing
made that was made.

JOHN 1:3

In him was life, and the life
was the light of men.

JOHN 1:4

The light shines in the darkness, and
the darkness has not overcome it.

JOHN 1:5

Portraits

Have you ever stared at a piece of art and wondered what message the artist was trying to convey?

In a painting there can be hints of a bigger picture or message. The same is true with God's Word. Throughout Scripture we find shadows revealing the presence of Jesus in the word-portraits created by the Master Artist Himself.

Physically speaking, <u>shadows prove the sun is shining</u>. The sun shines and creates a shadow confirming someone or something is standing in the light. So, <u>the shadow is evidence of light</u> and the physical presence of a person or object. But shadows aren't as detailed as the real person or object. Shadows give us a shape but not a complete picture.

Spiritually speaking, the portrait-shadows we find in the Old Testament reflect versions and variations of Jesus. But just like physical shadows, these "shadows of Jesus" only partially reflect Jesus.

Bible scholars call this typology. Essentially, each of these portraits paints an image or characteristic of Jesus, and understanding these "types" helps us see the purpose and work of Jesus in clarity and fulfillment in the New Testament.

Tracing the history of God's people throughout the Old Testament, we'll find that Adam, Eve, Moses, Joshua, David and Esther are all portraits that point to Jesus. Though they were imperfect with human flaws and frailties, each of these figures in Scripture, at times, did good works in their assignments. In that good, we find glimpses of a greater good that Jesus would eventually bring and complete.

It is our prayer that through each glimpse you see how Jesus will eventually right the wrongs and reveal His radiance as the light behind every shadow because He is the Son of God.

Adam and Eve

GENESIS 1–2; LUKE 3:21–38

*So God created mankind in his own image, in the image of God
he created them; male and female he created them.*

GENESIS 1:27

To begin to see Jesus in the Bible, the first place to look is Adam.

The Bible reveals important details about Adam. First, Adam and his wife, Eve, were created in the likeness and image of God and put in a beautiful place called the Garden of Eden. In Genesis 1–3, we read the following key moments in Adam and Eve's lives. Together, they were . . .

- given "*dominion*" over creation (Genesis 1:26).
- told to "*Be fruitful and multiply and fill the earth*" (Genesis 1:28b).
- told to "*subdue*" the land (Genesis 1:28b).
- told to "*keep*" the land (Genesis 2:15).
- told not to eat the fruit (Genesis 2:17).
- tempted by the serpent; they ate the fruit, and sin entered the world (Genesis 3:1–13).

All of the details surrounding the roles and responsibilities of Adam and Eve tell us God created humanity with dignity (being made in the image of God). That dignity came with a destiny (multiply, be fruitful, subdue, have dominion, keep/guard). This may be one of the most important things for us to remember not just as we look at the lives of Adam and Eve—but also as we wake up each morning and step into our day . . . Our dignity precedes our destiny.

01 How does knowing you're made in the likeness and image of God reassure you in a situation you're facing right now?

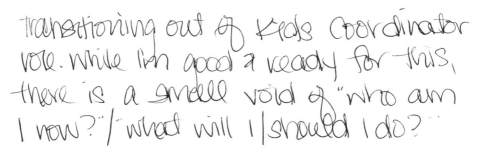

Transitioning out of Kids Coordinator role. While I'm good & ready for this, there is a small void of "who am I now?"/ what will I/should I do?

To be made in the likeness and image of God also had royal connotations. The language of the Ancient Near East would describe Adam and Eve as *viceregents,* meaning they were living as actual representatives of God Himself on earth. To be a viceregent is to reflect God's Kingship on earth.[2] This means Adam and Eve, and therefore all of humanity, were freely given the gift of dignity, wrapped up in royal privilege that came with royal expectations.

02 Read 1 Peter 2:9. What connection do you see between Adam and Eve having a royal identity and God calling us as believers "*a royal priesthood*"?

We are both "chosen" to show ∅ to others.

The expectations for Adam and Eve are seen clearly in Genesis 2:15 where God takes man and woman and places them in the Garden of Eden to "*work it and* keep *it*" (emphasis added). The English word "keep" is a translation of the Hebrew word "*shamar,*" which can be, and often is, translated as "guard or protect."[3]

The implication of this word used for Adam and Eve in Eden meant that they were not just to be gardeners working the fields. No, they were also priests who had guarding and protecting duties. Sadly, this is also what is unfulfilled in their actions. Adam and Eve fail to "*shamar,*" or guard and protect, Eden from the serpent, and they themselves are led into deception.

03 Read Genesis 3 and record what stands out to you about Adam and Eve's conversation and overall interaction with the serpent.

A consistent theme we will turn to in this study is that Jesus is *better*. Jesus is the better Adam and Eve because Jesus faces the situations of temptation, but He is found as the faithful Son of God. Sadly, Adam and Eve fall short in their faith. However, Jesus will never fall short. Jesus will never get distracted by sin. He will never betray or abandon you. He will never stop guarding and protecting you.

04 How does this truth about Jesus' faithfulness encourage you in what you're walking through right now?

Let's return to that list of key moments in the lives of Adam and Eve and look for a connection with Jesus:

Adam and Eve were given dominion over creation, but Jesus is the creator and sustainer of all things.

All things were made through Christ and for Christ (John 1:3; Colossians 1:16), and it is through Christ that all things are sustained (Colossians 1:15–17). This should give us such immense confidence. Jesus not only cares for creation but is very present in creation: He was there in Genesis 1, and He is here now.

You may be facing some situations now where Jesus seems absent. There is chaos and confusion. Hurt and heartbreak. Divorce and disease. These are awful circumstances, but they are not evidence that Jesus doesn't care. These are all realities in a world where sin exists.

Jesus is not a distracted king letting the world fall apart while He stands as an inactive bystander. He is the solution to the sin that's destroying people. Jesus wants us to see Him as the solution and to experience His presence and His kindness even in the middle of all that we're experiencing right now.

Adam and Eve were told to *"Be fruitful and multiply and fill the earth"* **(Genesis 1:28b).**

This assignment from God is for image bearers (people made in the image of God) to fill the earth with evidence of God's goodness and God's faithfulness. Sin disrupted perfection, but sin did not destroy this God-given assignment.

We see a connection here to the same instruction Jesus gives us in the New Testament found in Matthew 28:19. Some of Jesus' last instructions were to go and *"make disciples of all nations."* Isn't this fascinating? Adam and Eve received a similar command as the disciples received from Jesus . . . and those same instructions still apply to us today.

05   Can you think of ways you can obey Jesus' command to "make disciples of all nations"?

Adam and Eve were tempted by the serpent and ate the fruit, which ushered in sin. But Jesus conquered the power of the serpent and provided freedom from sin.

If there is one thing the enemy capitalizes upon, it's tempting us when we least expect it. It's something he's been working on since Genesis 3 where he successfully tempted Adam and Eve, which led to a rupture in relationship with God, creation, and God's people.

In the Gospels, we find Jesus in a similar predicament where He is tempted by Satan. But just before Jesus is tempted, we find Him in what may have been the most epic moment of His earthly life and ministry (Matthew 3:13–17; Mark 1:9–11; Luke 3:21–22). His baptism

After Jesus is baptized by John the Baptist, God the Father says to Jesus, *"You are my beloved Son; with you I am well pleased"* (Luke 3:22). Let's not skip this moment or overlook its significance. Right before Jesus is led in the wilderness to be tempted by Satan (the same serpent in Genesis 3), God the Father publicly affirms and confirms Him.

Not many would go to the wilderness willingly. The wilderness, for the Israelites, and even for us today, represents isolation and hardship. For Jesus, going into the wilderness of a physical desert meant treacherous dangers like wild animals and no guarantees of water supply. Yet Jesus was led into the wilderness where He would prove Himself to be the better and greater Adam.

Jesus was tempted, but unlike Adam and Eve, He was not deceived. Jesus used the words of Scripture and showed us how powerful Truth is against the enemy's schemes. Adam and Eve knew God's words but lacked the trust to follow His instructions when their own desires seemed more appealing.

Because of Jesus, everything changed. The ruptured relationship between God and His people, caused by sin, was repaired in Christ. And as we have learned today, Jesus isn't just the better and greater Adam; He is the Savior King.

Moses

EXODUS 1–2; MATTHEW 1:18–2:15

———

He is the image of the invisible God, the firstborn of all creation. For by him all things were created, in heaven and on earth, visible and invisible, whether thrones or dominions or rulers or authorities—all things were created through him and for him.

COLOSSIANS 1:15–16

When you think about the Old Testament and the "founding fathers" of our faith, who comes to mind for you? I still remember being a little girl watching Charlton Heston, dressed in a red robe, with wild gray hair, hold up his arms and part the Red Sea. I was even more mesmerized when I found out this account of Moses was a true story.

I think many of us would say that Moses is one of the most important biblical figures in the Old Testament (possibly tied with David, whom we will also look at this week).

Historically, Moses is believed to be the author of the first five books of the Old Testament. He's a unique prophet of God who actually meets with the Lord face to face. When reading about the life of Moses, we find important similarities in the life of Jesus as well. Let's take a look at some of those:

First, both the mother of Jesus and the mother of Moses acted in courageous and selfless ways to ensure the safety and security of their sons. Jesus and Moses had such unusual beginnings to their lives.

01   Read Exodus 1–2. What stands out to you about the birth and early life of Moses?

+Shiphrah & Puah's willingness to defy King's orders
+Moses' parents were able to keep him hidden for 3 months!
+Pharaoh's daughter wanted to keep him
+G orchestrated that his mother could spend more time with him
+Moses was able to escape Pharaoh's attempt to kill him

02   Read Matthew 1:18–2:15. What similarities do you see in the birth of Jesus after reading about the birth of Moses?

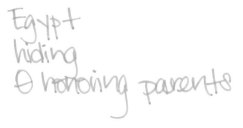

Egypt
hiding
⊖ honoring parents

Second, Moses and Jesus both had assignments to lead people out of enslavement. Moses led the Israelites out of the bondage of Pharaoh and Egypt. But Jesus would eventually lead all of those who place their faith in Him out of a bondage worse than that of Pharaoh—the grip of sin and death.

• What Moses begins for the people of God, Jesus fulfills forever for the family of God.

At the end of Exodus 3 and the beginning of Exodus 4, God called Moses to represent Him to Pharaoh in order to release and free the Israelites. But Moses had to convince more than Pharaoh. First, Moses had to convince the Israelites that it was time to leave their bondage and captivity.

Moses responded by saying, *"But behold, they will not believe me or listen to my voice . . ."* (Exodus 4:1).

It's important to note that earlier, in Exodus 2:15, Moses had already tried to help the Israelites, but they essentially turned on him. So what's the key difference between Exodus 2 and Exodus 4?

In Exodus 2, Moses was trying to achieve something for his people out of his own might and work. However, now in Exodus 4, Moses was no longer working in his own strength and wisdom. He was being appointed and led by God.

When we look deeper into Exodus 4:1–17, we find Moses so focused on his weaknesses that he forgets God's power.

03   Look at the words of Moses in Exodus 4:1; 4:10; and 4:13. Why do you think Moses responded in this way?

"What if they don't believe me?"
"I'm not good with words."
"Send someone else."
+Doubting himself

Where Moses says *"but . . . they will . . ."* (v. 1) and *"I am not . . ."* (v. 10), God responds with *"I will be"* (vv. 12, 15). Moses disqualified himself, but God reminded Moses not of what disqualified him but of who was mighty with him: God Himself. God was the one who equipped Moses with the signs necessary to gain the trust of the Israelites. Though Moses angered God by asking Him to send someone else, God also provided Aaron to comfort and ease the anxiety of Moses.

In spite of the fact that God called Moses, Moses let his doubts and insecurities feed a distrust of God. And so often the same is true for us. Whether our trust issues are rooted in internal insecurities and insufficiencies or external obstacles that make us afraid, God reveals Himself as *"I will be."* This is our promise to hang on to in the middle of our own trust issues.

04   What assignment has God put before you today where you're struggling to trust in Him fully?

+ New friendships

+ A place for me (next job)

As we consider Moses' assignment, we see God never told him to bring the power. Moses was simply told to bring the words and be obedient. God's job was everything else: the power, the strategy, the plans, and certainly the victory. The same is true for you and me. We can be encouraged, knowing He will lead us with what to say, what to do, and how to move forward.

We all have some trust issues, thankfully Jesus models the better way for us to handle our doubt when we are faced with a difficult assignment or even suffering in circumstances we didn't cause. We see this so beautifully lived out in Matthew 26:36–39 in the Garden of Gethsemane. Jesus displayed the perfect example of crying out to God in complete distress in His humanity, but He immediately backed it up with *". . . nevertheless, not as I will, but as you will"* (Matthew 26:39).

"learned obedience through what he suffered."

(HEBREWS 5:8)

05   What surprises you about this verse? What encourages you about it?

The obedience of Moses created greater trust in God, and the outcome was the liberation of God's people. This paints a beautiful shadow portrait of expectation for the greater Moses: Jesus. Jesus' life of obedience ultimately led Him to the cross for the liberation of humanity from sin and death. What a gift God gave us in knowing the story of Moses so we could see in an earthly sense what Jesus accomplished in an eternal sense.

He was "I Am" for Moses, and He was "I Am" through Jesus. And He will be "I Am" in whatever you're facing right now, too.

Joshua

———

I am the good shepherd. The good shepherd lays down his life for the sheep.

JOHN 10:11

Yesterday we talked a lot about trust and obedience. I've found in my own life that the more I trust God, the more I will choose to do things His way. But it's also true that the more we obey, the more we learn to trust Him. Trust and obedience go hand in hand.

God promised to care for His people, but they must trust and obey Him. Today, we'll take a look at Joshua, a man known for his extraordinary trust and obedience.

Because of that trust, God appointed Joshua to lead the Israelites into the promised land and God's promised rest. And as we'll see today, Joshua's leadership and obedience to God provide a portrait of Jesus who through His perfect obedience, leads us into perfect rest.

There are many similarities between Joshua and Jesus, starting with their names. In English, their names are different. But "Jesus" and "Joshua" come from the same root name. One scholar has said, "Jesus was named after Joshua."[4] This becomes important in the book of Hebrews as the connection between Joshua and Jesus is established.

But let's take a closer look at Joshua and his responsibility.

Tragically, Moses was unable to enter the promised land because of his disobedience and lack of faith. Knowing the Israelites would need a leader, Moses asked the Lord to appoint a shepherd in his place. Moses worried, *"who shall go out before them and come in before them, who shall lead them out and bring them in, that the congregation of the LORD may not be as sheep that have no shepherd"* (Numbers 27:17).

A shepherd's responsibility was to lead the sheep to green pastures so they could rest. Joshua, as the "shepherd" of the Israelites, was tasked with the important responsibility to lead them into the green pastures and rest of the promised land.

Joshua was appointed to be a type of "shepherd," but John 10:11 tells us that, even more so, Jesus embodies this for us: "I am the good shepherd. The good shepherd lays down his life for the sheep."

While Joshua led the people to physical rest, Jesus' presence offers us rest for our souls: *"Come to me, all who labor and are heavy laden, and I will give you rest. Take my yoke upon you, and learn from me, for I am gentle and lowly in heart, and you will find rest for your souls"* (Matthew 11:28–29).

01   Thinking about your current needs and circumstances, how might you begin to see more of Jesus as your Good Shepherd leading you to rest?

Joshua did lead the Israelites into the promised land where they expected rest. But when they arrived in Canaan (their promised land), all was not as they hoped. We can all relate to the Israelites in being surprised by problems that come with our version of "promised lands."

02   Have you ever hoped for something, but when it finally arrived, it was different than what you expected? How did this affect you?

Joshua

Jesus

NAME

Yehoshua

Joshua comes from the Hebrew name "Yehoshua," meaning "Yahweh is deliverance," "God is deliverance."

NAME

Yeshua/Y'shua

The name Jesus is derived from the Hebrew name, which is based on the Semitic root *y-sh-'* (Hebrew: ישע), meaning "to deliver; to rescue."

APPOINTMENT

Joshua, as the "shepherd" of the Israelites, was tasked with the important responsibility to lead them into the green pastures and rest of the promised land.

APPOINTMENT

"I am the good shepherd. The good shepherd lays down his life for the sheep."

John 10:11

ACTION

Joshua led the people to promised physical rest in their earthly inheritance of Canaan.

ACTION

"Come to me, all who labor and are heavy laden, and I will give you rest."

Matthew 11:28

STRUGGLE

Led people who disobeyed. Could not deliver people from sin.

STRUGGLE

Loved people in their disobedience. Gave His life for their sins.

Joshua led the people faithfully into their earthly inheritance of Canaan, but they never ultimately experienced the rest they hoped for, due to their disobedience to God. They worshipped and followed after false gods, bringing the consequences upon themselves. (See Deuteronomy 11:26–29.)

So, though God kept His promise and honored the people, the people didn't honor Him in return. And sadly, we do this very same thing. We long for peace and rest but often don't do what God says . . . or we suffer because others around us don't do what God says. In both cases, the result is unrest.

Another connection between Joshua and Jesus is they were both faithful but led people with a propensity toward disobedience. And though Joshua was obedient in his assignment, he could not deliver the people from sin. Thankfully, Jesus provides what Joshua never could: forgiveness of our sins and rest for our souls *even in* hard circumstances and pain.

Joshua only did in part what Jesus would later do in full. Joshua was a good shepherd, but Jesus is the Great Shepherd (Hebrews 13:20), leading His people into eternal security and peace with Him, through His death, burial, resurrection, and ascension into heaven.

But how is Jesus our Great Shepherd today if He's no longer physically present with us? The Holy Spirit, or the Spirit of Jesus, is inside of us as believers. When Jesus was here on earth, His physical presence with people was limited to whoever He was with at that moment. But when Jesus ascended into heaven, He promised the gift of His Spirit would be with all believers all the time.

THE HOLY SPIRIT IS REFERRED TO IN DIFFERENT
WAYS THROUGHOUT SCRIPTURE.

The Spirit of God

EPHESIANS 4:30

The Holy Spirit

EPHESIANS 1:13

The Spirit of Christ

ROMANS 8:9

03   Jesus is present and within us through the Spirit. Read Philippians 1:19; Acts 16:7; and Galatians 4:6 and reflect upon their meaning. Write some of the truths contained within these Scripture verses that stand out to you.

The journey to the promised land was not an easy one. Nor was Jesus' road to the cross and our salvation easy. They were both difficult roads paved with tragedy and turmoil. They were filled with obstacles that seemed to shout, "Your God is not for you. Just look around you! This sure doesn't look like the road to fulfilled promises to me."

Maybe you're in a place like that right now. You're trying to cling to the promises of God and move forward in faith, but difficult circumstances seem to be shouting loudly in opposition. Perhaps your difficult situation is daring you to doubt the goodness of God . . . inviting you to label Him forgetful or even unfair . . . tempting you to panic and give up hope.

We've all walked through seasons where our circumstances don't seem to line up with God's promises. But just because they don't line up doesn't mean God isn't going to show up.

Because of Jesus, we can have peace and rest right where we are today. He is our peace. He is our rest. Peace and rest for our souls isn't a physical journey we must take but rather they are a spiritual practice of trust we get to participate in today.

04   Read Matthew 11:28–30. How do these words provide comfort during difficult times?

Oh, friend, our God is a God of completion. He makes promises, and then He fulfills them (Hebrews 10:23). Yes, the journey may be harder than we expected. The road to our promise may not look anything like we thought it would. But we can rest assured there is never a question of whether or not our God will be faithful.

Jesus is evidence of His faithfulness to us! We can trust Him. Even when life takes unexpected twists and turns. Our God is a promise-keeping God.

David

1 SAMUEL 16:7; ACTS 13:22

. . . behold, wise men from the east came to Jerusalem, saying,
"Where is he who has been born king of the Jews?"

MATTHEW 2:1B–2A

Have you ever wanted something so badly that you'd do almost anything to get it? Maybe you've overlooked red flags, pushed through resistance and carried on despite warnings. I've often thought that my way was the best way without really considering God's way.

01   How do you personally relate to wanting solutions to circumstances more than trusting God's instructions and heeding His warnings?

After being freed from Egypt, wandering in the wilderness, and coming against numerous tests and trials, the Israelites, led by Joshua, eventually entered the promised land. After this came a period when judges served as leaders of the Israelites, but what the people longed for was a true king to lead them.

They'd observed the ways of the pagan nations around them who had physical, human rulers sitting on a throne, and Israel longed for something that was never intended for them. We know they already had a king—Yahweh—but the Israelites continued to look for ways to have their needs met outside of God.

"YAHWEH" IS THE INTIMATE NAME OF GOD FOR THE ISRAELITES;
IT WAS A NAME THAT REMINDED THE PEOPLE OF THE GREATNESS OF GOD
AND THAT THEY WERE HIS POSSESSION AND INHERITANCE.
(DEUTERONOMY 4:19–20; 32:8–9)[5]

Longings are complicated feelings. They are desires with an intensity and drive behind them that feel urgent to resolve. When our motives are pure and our hearts are in a good place, we are more likely to trust God even when we don't understand His timing. But, when we are disoriented or in an unhealthy place, our longings can become misdirected. We end up seeking things that have the false promise of fulfillment and satisfaction but only bring more confusion, deeper bondage, and entrapment.[6]

02   Read God's warning in 1 Samuel 8:10–18. How would a human king treat the people?

Despite God's warnings against an earthly king, the Israelites wanted what they wanted. The people didn't consider that a human king is still very human. They discovered this truth when their first king, Saul, stopped relying on God, and protected his position more than helping the people.

God chose David to be the next leader of Israel. Not only was David appointed, but he actually became the "ideal king" that all other kings were compared to throughout the books of 1 and 2 Kings.[7]

God's Ideal King

LIVES IN FULL SUBMISSION TO
THE KING OF HEAVEN AND EARTH.

HAS A HEART FOR GOD
MORE THAN ACCOMPLISHMENT.

LEADS ALL PEOPLE BY EXAMPLE
TO PURSUE HOLINESS AND GOD.

David exemplified these aspects of kingship. David knew who the true King was, and he made obeying God and honoring God's ways his priority.

We also see David's patience and trust in God's timing. Before David was appointed king, Saul became jealous and tried to kill him. David could have easily justified taking revenge and claiming the throne before his time. Instead, yielding to God's will, he left Saul in God's hands and didn't retaliate.

David trusted God in such a similar way to Jesus. When Jesus' life was being threatened just before He went to the cross, He prayed, *"not what I will, but what you will"* in Mark 14:36c.

Learning to trade my will for God's will has made such a shift in my perspective and brought so much peace. Instead of always trying to solve my problems myself and ask God to bless my suggestions, I've decided to pray out loud, "I'm trading my will for Thy will because I'm so confident You will, God."

03   Is there an area of your life where God has asked you to trade your will for His? Write down what God might be asking you to submit.

In David we find a king who understands he serves under the great King and does so faithfully because of the condition of his heart.

04   Read 1 Samuel 16:7. What do you see further explained about the condition of our hearts? How does this speak to you?

05   What else do we learn about the condition of David's heart in 1 Samuel 13:14 and Acts 13:22?

The heart posture of King David is what gave his kingship value and worth. The title of king itself was meaningless without a heart attuned to God. However, even though David's heart was yielded to God, his life was still complicated. For all the good he did, he also caused some immense damage to himself, his family, and even the kingdom of Israel because of his sins.

As great of a king as David was, the one victory he could not win was the victory over sin. Only Jesus could fill the gap that sin created between God and man. Remember, we've examined before that these figures in the Bible were portraits of Jesus, but they were always imperfect. They could only do in part what Jesus could do in perfection.

David

How We See Him	How God Saw Him
Had a married woman brought to him to sleep with, Bathsheba. (2 Samuel 11:1–5)	A man after His own heart. (1 Samuel 13:14; Acts 13:22)
Murdered Uriah, Bathsheba's husband, when she became pregnant with David's child. (2 Samuel 11:6–27)	Responded to sin with humility David said to Nathan, "I have sinned against the LORD." (2 Samuel 12:13)
Trusted his own might over God and took a census of Israel. (1 Chronicles 21:1; 21:8)	Willing confessor "For I know my transgressions and my sin is ever before me." (Psalm 51:3)
Broke the Law by having more than one wife as prescribed for the king. (Deuteronomy 17:17)	Example of true repentance "For you will not delight in sacrifice, or I would give it; you will not be pleased with a burnt offering. The sacrifices of God are a broken spirit; a broken and contrite heart, O God, you will not despise." (Psalm 51:16–17; 2 Samuel 22:24–26)

David experienced deep pain as a result of his sin, but his story still provides encouragement and hope for us. It displays tragedy and brokenness but shows that God can still work for good in the midst of it all. And best of all, God didn't leave David on his own to figure it out.

06 No matter our past, we can choose today to be a people after God's own heart—placing our faith in Jesus, humbly choosing to own our sin, repent and let God's grace and forgiveness flood in. Look at the phrases below and circle which ones you need to tend to today and commit to act.
- Owning my sin.
- Repenting out of true brokenness.
- Not blaming others or justifying what I've done.
- Not making excuses for sinful behaviors I know I need to stop.
- Not minimizing or covering up what I've done.
- Receiving God's grace and forgiveness.
- Giving God's grace and forgiveness to another.

As we end today, write out a prayer thanking Jesus for being our ultimate King who holds the keys of victory over sin and death yesterday, today, and forevermore.

Esther

—

And we have seen and testify that the Father has sent his Son to be the Savior of the world.

1 JOHN 4:14

What if I told you that we can actually find Jesus in the book of Esther? You might not remember seeing Him in those pages before, but He's there.

Today we'll see that Esther is a great book for us to establish our footing in the unexpected, unseen, and sometimes completely upside-down nature of life.

Esther is an uncommon book in the Bible. It's only one of two books named after a woman, the other being Ruth. Additionally, the name of God isn't found in the text, and Esther omits important common biblical themes like the Sinai covenant, Israelite traditions, Jerusalem, the temple, and the land of Israel.

BUT LET'S CONSIDER WHAT
IS PRESENT IN ESTHER:

heartbreaking circumstances, complicated relationship dynamics, unexpected betrayal, and people who are just flat-out mean.

These details make the story of Esther relevant to what many of us face today, when it can seem like Jesus is missing. And yet, as we are learning, Jesus is never absent.

Jesus experienced the feelings of humanity in His perfect divinity. He knew overwhelming sorrow and the brutality of betrayal (John 11:32–35; Luke 19:41–44). He knows what we are experiencing, and His presence will change us in the midst of our circumstances.

01   How does this bring you comfort in what you're facing today?

Before we examine the portrait of Jesus in the life of Esther, let's look for the presence of God in her story.

- Though Esther was both an orphan and a Jew, *somehow* Esther was picked for the royal court and given special consideration from Hegai, who was in charge of the women. (Esther 2)
- *At just the right time,* Mordecai, Esther's cousin, discovered a plot to overthrow the king and told Esther (Esther 2:19–23).
- Haman, a Persian court official, saw Mordecai refuse to bow to him and had murder in his heart, not just for Mordecai but for all the Jews (Esther 3:4–6). It seemed like this turn of events works in favor of evil, *but not for long.*
- Mordecai asked Esther to speak on behalf of her people. Esther, who made the *unlikely journey* into the royal court, had direct access to the king at this pivotal time. (Esther 4)
- *The king couldn't sleep one night* and had an assistant read all the accounts of people who had done "memorable deeds." *Of all the accounts,* the king heard Mordecai's story and desired to honor Mordecai (Esther 6).
- The king asked Hamen for his opinion on how to honor Mordecai. *In irony,* Haman answered the king and then had to lead Mordecai around in a procession in his honor (Esther 6).
- In a last-ditch effort, Haman built gallows for Mordecai. But after Esther exposed Haman's evil plot, *Haman was hanged on his own gallows* (Esther 5:9–14; 7:5–10).

The Chronology of God's Presence in Esther's Story

JEW

ORPHAN

LIFTED HER COUSIN
MORDECAI TO
STATE OF ESTEEM
ESTHER 10

MIRACULOUS
PLOT FOR DEATH
THWARTED INTO
VICTORY
ESTHER 5:9–14;
7:5–10

CHOSEN BY HEGAI
(IN CHARGE OF
KING'S WOMEN)
ESTHER 2

COUSIN MORDECAI
FOUND HONOR
WITH THE KING
ESTHER 6

GIVEN SPECIFIC
INSIGHT
ESTHER 2:19–23

SPOKE UP ON
BEHALF OF ALL JEWS
ESTHER 4

DIRECT ACCESS
TO THE KING
ESTHER 4

ESTHER

Look at all of the statements that are italicized on page 38. There are so many more examples, but these moments reveal the presence and provision of God. In the story of Esther, the twists and turns are not coincidental. The same is true in our lives. God's presence may be unseen, but He is still working.

02   Where are you being challenged to have faith in God's "unseen" activity right now?

Now let's look at the portrait of Jesus through Esther and her life. During the times of Esther and Jesus, the people believed God had stopped speaking to them and acting on their behalf. Esther disrupted that period of silence. But Jesus ended it completely. In both situations, we see silence is not proof of the absence of God; it's proof that God is working in ways we can't see or hear.

WHEN MATTHEW 1 BEGINS,
THE PEOPLE OF GOD HAVE EXPERIENCED

"400 years of silence,"

THE PERIOD OF TIME BETWEEN THE END OF MALACHI
(THE LAST BOOK OF THE OLD TESTAMENT)
AND THE BEGINNING THE NEW TESTAMENT.

The birth of Jesus ended that silence.

Both Esther and Jesus entered human history in a time of great need. Esther was sent to save the Jewish people of her time. Jesus was sent to save all of humanity for eternity. Again, through this story of Esther, we get to see a human situation play out that shows us a glimpse in the physical realm of what Jesus is doing in the spiritual realm.

In both stories we find similarities:

THERE WAS AN EVIL PLAN.

THERE WAS AN ENEMY.

INNOCENT PEOPLE NEEDED SAVING.

AN UNEXPECTED HERO CAME FROM HUMBLE BEGINNINGS.

THE HERO REMAINED HUMBLE AND HONORED GOD.

THE HERO WAS UNIQUELY POSITIONED BY GOD TO FULFILL HIS PLAN.

THE HERO SET ASIDE WHAT WAS BEST FOR HIM FOR A GREATER PURPOSE.

03   Has God ever reversed a bad situation for your good? Write a short testimony of God's faithfulness.

TO CLOSE TODAY'S TEACHING AND THIS WEEK OF PORTRAITS, LET'S LOOK AT THE CORRELATION BETWEEN ESTHER AND JESUS THROUGH THE LENSES OF "SHADOW" AND "SUN."

Every shadow reminds us that something brighter and bigger exists.

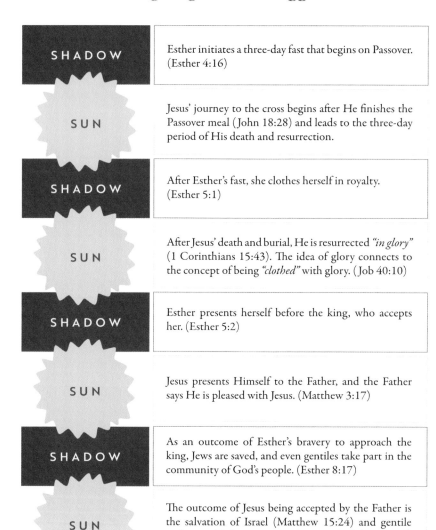

SHADOW

Esther initiates a three-day fast that begins on Passover. (Esther 4:16)

SUN

Jesus' journey to the cross begins after He finishes the Passover meal (John 18:28) and leads to the three-day period of His death and resurrection.

SHADOW

After Esther's fast, she clothes herself in royalty. (Esther 5:1)

SUN

After Jesus' death and burial, He is resurrected *"in glory"* (1 Corinthians 15:43). The idea of glory connects to the concept of being *"clothed"* with glory. (Job 40:10)

SHADOW

Esther presents herself before the king, who accepts her. (Esther 5:2)

SUN

Jesus presents Himself to the Father, and the Father says He is pleased with Jesus. (Matthew 3:17)

SHADOW

As an outcome of Esther's bravery to approach the king, Jews are saved, and even gentiles take part in the community of God's people. (Esther 8:17)

SUN

The outcome of Jesus being accepted by the Father is the salvation of Israel (Matthew 15:24) and gentile inclusion. (Colossians 2:11; Acts 11:18; Galatians 3:8)

*Father God, I praise You today for how far You
have carried me in my life. I'm so grateful today for
the gift of Your Son, Jesus. Thank You for the ways
You are opening my eyes and allowing me to see
Jesus in a whole new light. I pray for a discerning
mind and tender heart as I lean in to what You
may have for me. God, I trust You. I know that
You were never absent for a single moment in
Scripture, and You're never absent in my story,
either. I praise You today for the fact that, no
matter what I face, I will never be alone.
In Jesus' Name, Amen.*

Prophecies

Prophecy was used by God so the people could see something either in the present or the future.

Sometimes a prophecy had an *immediate fulfillment* that would boost people's confidence in God. Other times, the prophets spoke of things that wouldn't be fulfilled for hundreds of years, or longer. Then, there were also bifocal types of prophecies where a portion would be fulfilled sooner, and an additional part would be fulfilled later.

When it comes to the prophecies specifically telling of the coming Messiah (also known as messianic prophecies), we find both the distant-future type of prophecies and the bifocal types of prophecies. In fact, just like we learned last week about portraits that were *shadows* of the coming Christ, these prophecies work in a similar way. Prophecies are like a shadow pointing to a future and final fulfillment of *when* Jesus would eventually come and *what* He would eventually fulfill.

Understanding the Term "Prophecy"

PROPHECY (NOUN)
A message concerning future events and how they relate to people.

PROPHESY (VERB)
The act or occurrence of prophecy being shared or announced.

MESSIANIC PROPHECY
A future promise that is specific to the promised Messiah (who we know is Jesus) coming in the flesh as the King who will bring justice and ultimately right all of the wrongs that result from sin.

PROPHET
The vessel to whom God would speak directly and who would convey the prophecies to other people.

MAJOR PROPHETS
Isaiah, Jeremiah, Lamentations, Ezekiel, and Daniel.
- Books in Old Testament
- Longer and focus on broader themes and topics (ex: holiness).

MINOR PROPHETS
Hosea, Joel, Amos, Obadiah, Jonah, Micah, Nahum, Habakkuk, Zephaniah, Haggai, Zechariah, and Malachi.
- Referred to as "The 12."
- Shorter and more narrowly focused (ex: focus in Joel on the coming of the Holy Spirit).

The idea of prophesy was quite familiar to the Israelites in the Old Testament. The pagan nations surrounding Israel used magic and divination as a means of conjuring up "prophecy" or seeing into the future. The Israelites were forbidden to practice this kind of magic. But they had prophets. And it wasn't unusual for them to receive, through a prophet, a message from God about the future.

Although God had already spoken to the Israelites through the Law (God's commands for His people to live by), He also spoke through prophecy when there was a timely message related to a specific event for the people of Israel. The origin and source of the message was God, but He used prophets to communicate to His people.

The prophets played a major role in the history of God's people. Some of the prophets saw a once-mighty kingdom divide into two kingdoms, then finally collapse and be overtaken by foreign nations. This devastation was something they would have never expected, but it happened before their own eyes. Because they lived in times that were hard, the people were desperate for messages from God.

Some of the prophets lived during a time period called the "Exile" when the Israelites were held in captivity by the Babylonians and Assyrians. This was a time of hopelessness, sorrow, and pain. The promises of God were still present but seemed far away and out of reach.

Finally, the "Postexilic" period was when the people of God were allowed to go back to their land and rebuild the temple, their walls, their city, and homes. But what they rebuilt didn't compare to the previous temple and the glory of the city at the time of David and Solomon.

EGYPT	ASSYRIA

NORTHERN AND SOUTHERN KINGDOMS	JUDAH

▲ SOLOMON DIES

▲ ISRAEL FALLS

major prophets

ISAIAH

Once-mighty kingdom divides into two kingdoms

minor prophets

OBADIAH

JOEL

JONAH

AMOS

HOSEA

MICAH

other prophets & OT books

ELIJAH

ELISHA

650	600	550	500	450	400

BABYLON   PERSIA

ALONE	EXILE	POST-EXILE

▲ JUDAH FALLS

▲ CAPTIVES RETURN

Nothing compared to original previous temple and glory of Jerusalem during King David and Solomon

JEREMIAH/LAMENTATIONS

DANIEL

EZEKIEL

The people were desperate for messages from God

NAHUM   HAGGAI   MALACHI

ZEPHANIAH   ZECHARIAH

HABAKUK

Promises of God were still present but seemed far away and out of reach

ESTHER

EZRA

NEHEMIAH

These historical moments are not just a back-then reality. They relate to our right-now experiences. Maybe you can understand the feeling of seeing something you've invested your heart and soul in shift from being strong and secure to being divided and in ruins.

Or maybe you feel like you're in the very center of the wilderness. It feels like exile . . . nothing is going right and it's been that way for a while. All of your hopes and dreams for the future feel out of reach and you are desperate to hear from God.

Maybe there are other situations where you are in a rebuilding process. You've gathered broken pieces of that part of your life and proclaimed that the Lord is redeemer over it all. You've started looking for the good things God will surely work from all of this brokenness, but it's taking a lot of time.

Friend, the prophecies that told of the coming Messiah took place in similar situations and circumstances. These prophecies reveal promises that still reign true today. And though we have the benefit now of living in the reality of a Messiah who has already come, we still long for the day He will return.

He was. He is. And He will forever be the Redeemer King.

We have a bifocal promise of hope for today and hope for the future as we wait for complete redemption when Jesus returns. Old Testament scholar Christopher Wright says it this way: "The Old Testament tells the story that Jesus completes."[8]

This week, we will discover prophecies that tell of the coming of Christ and things He would accomplish. May these revelations bring you even greater confidence in how much you are thought of and cared for by God.

He was. He is. And He will **forever be** the Redeemer King.

Prophesy in the Beginning

GENESIS 3 / LUKE 1

For everyone who has been born of God overcomes the world. And this is the victory that has overcome the world—our faith. Who is it that overcomes the world except the one who believes that Jesus is the Son of God?"

1 JOHN 5:4–5

The very first prophecy that Jesus would be born from a woman and of the future restoration He will bring is found in Genesis 3:15: *"I will put enmity between you and the woman, and between your offspring and her offspring; he shall bruise your head, and you shall bruise his heel."* Old Testament scholar Derek Kidner refers to this verse as "the first glimmer of the gospel."[9]

In the middle of Adam and Eve receiving the consequences of their sin and rebellion (also referred to as "the fall"), God promises that the woman and Satan will be enemies. God also brings judgment on the serpent, and it's in the punishment for his rebellious actions that we get a glimpse of what Jesus, the coming Messiah, will do to the evil one.

Though the enemy will bring pain to the woman's children, he will receive a much greater blow. Isn't it merciful of God to mention the future hope of what Jesus will do to the enemy in the midst of Adam and Eve's fear of all that was unfolding?!

01   What does this reveal to you personally about the mercy of God?

Genesis 3:15 is an example of the Law of First Mention.

THE LAW OF FIRST MENTION IS WHERE SOMETHING IS FIRST
SEEN OR FOUND (USUALLY IN THE OLD TESTAMENT) AND THEN
FULFILLED, COMPLETED AND/OR FURTHERED LATER IN SCRIPTURE.
LOOKING INTO THE VARIOUS MENTIONS HELPS US MORE CLEARLY
DEFINE AND UNDERSTAND BIBLICAL EVENTS AND TERMS. SO, HERE,
THE GOOD NEWS IS ANNOUNCED FOR THE FIRST TIME. AND LATER,
IN THE NEW TESTAMENT, IT IS FULFILLED.

02   Look up John 10:10 and write down what this verse reveals about the enemy and Jesus.

Three Components of the Genesis 3:15 Prophecy

THE SERPENT/SATAN

Unnamed in Genesis 3

The serpent was "crafty" (Genesis 3:1)

Had an agenda beyond Adam and Eve eating fruit

In Hebrew, the serpent goes from being a crafty *(arum)* serpent to becoming a cursed *(arur)* serpent (Genesis 3:14)[10]

POINT:
He intends to steal, kill, and destroy, but in the end, his craftiness leads to the curse and consequences he will bear

THE SEED OF THE SERPENT

"Offspring" in Genesis 3:15 is
the English translation of the
Hebrew word for "seed"

Used twice to refer to both the
seed of the woman and the seed of
the serpent Pharisees referred to as
children of the devil (John 8:44)

Pharisees considered themselves
children of Abraham (John 8:39)

DEFINITION:
All those who follow the ways and works of
Satan, the great, deceiving, ancient serpent
(see Revelation 12:9)

THE SEED OF THE WOMAN

Debated among Old Testament
scholars. There is a dispute as to
whether the "seed" should be
understood as individual or collective

INDIVIDUAL:
the promised Messiah / the individual
person of Jesus because Jesus came from
the lineage of Eve

COLLECTIVE:
all of humanity that will come from Eve for
generations to come, including us today /
all those who put their faith and trust
in Jesus

03   Take a look at 1 John 3:7–10. What do these verses tell us are the distinguishing marks of being a child (seed) of God versus a child (seed) of Satan?

04   Read Galatians 3:16 in either the NIV or CSB translation. What word do you see pop up again?

What we see revealed in Galatians is not an "either/or" situation but a "both/and." The "seed" is individual, but the seed is also collective because in Jesus the Church is formed.

In Galatians 3:16, the Apostle Paul looks back on Genesis 3:15 and identifies the promised "seed" as Christ, furthering the promise made to Abraham. Abraham's offspring includes all people who put their faith in Jesus—also known as the Church! This represents the "Collective Descendants" as well. (See Romans 4:13; Romans 4:16–18; Galatians 3:8.)

And when God says *"he shall bruise your head, and you shall bruise his heel"* (Genesis 3:15), God prophesies that the offspring of the woman will *"bruise"* Satan's head, but Satan will *"bruise"* His heel. Though the enemy will try to derail God's mission to save the world through His Son, Jesus will claim ultimate victory over the serpent. And furthermore, that victory is a victory that the "Collective Descendants," or "Collective Seeds," of the Church share when we find ourselves *in Christ*.

"For everyone who has been born of God overcomes the world. And this is the victory that has overcome the world—our faith. Who is it that overcomes the world except the one who believes that Jesus is the Son of God?" (1 John 5:4–5)

05 How does knowing we share in the same victory as Christ encourage you? Where are you needing to see victory in your own life right now?

We have the benefit of being on the side of history that gets to flip to passages in the New Testament where we read of Jesus' life, death, burial, resurrection, and ascension. We get to celebrate the fulfillment that was *only prophesied* at the time of Genesis 3:15.

Even though we get this advantage of reading the complete story of the Bible today, it's important to remember that the hundreds of pages separating Genesis 3 and the New Testament in our Bibles represent thousands of years that people waited for the promised Messiah.

In this truth, we find one of the requirements for biblical prophecy: dependence on God. God wants our complete dependence on Him and trust in His timing to bring about what He has promised and prophesied. When we patiently wait on God it develops in us the endurance we need for our faith to be strong.

From Genesis through Malachi, the ancient people of God waited for the Messiah to come. Similarly, we await the return of Jesus to permanently rescue us from the hurt of this broken world and to establish the new heavens and new earth. Before then, we have the everyday reality of waiting for Jesus to intervene in some way.

. . . Waiting for Jesus to reveal to us our exact next step.
. . . Waiting to get married and start a family of our own.
. . . Waiting to get clear scans at that next doctor's appointment.
. . . Waiting for breakthroughs in complicated relationships.

When we find ourselves in a delay, we must determine to fill the gap between where we are now and where we want to be by remembering Jesus is with us, and intentionally looking for His activity.

What was only promised in Genesis 3:15 was fulfilled on the cross where Jesus conquered sin, death, and the enemy. And even in the middle of the tragedy of sin, God had Jesus in mind as the solution. Jesus has always been Plan A. And the next time the Messiah returns, He will do so not as a suffering servant but as the reigning, victorious King of heaven and earth.

But until then . . . we get the privilege of leaning into Jesus as we endure, patiently wait, and keep our faith in Him strong.

**When we
patiently wait
on God it
develops in us
the *endurance*
we need for our
faith to be strong.**

Prayers and Praise

1 SAMUEL 1; EPHESIANS 6:10–20

———

*And Hannah prayed and said, "My heart exults in the L*ORD*; my horn is exalted in the L*ORD*.*
My mouth derides my enemies, because I rejoice in your salvation."

1 SAMUEL 2:1

Have you ever prayed and waited for something while watching someone else get the very thing you've longed for? It's even more painful when that person flaunts their blessing in your face.

If anyone knows the heartbreak of patiently waiting while also enduring someone's cruelty, it was Hannah from 1 Samuel. Hannah desired to be a mother but continued day after day with no children.

01   Read 1 Samuel 1:1–8. Who is this story about, and what is the situation? Summarize in your own words.

THE TERM "RIVAL" (צָרָה *[TSARAH]*) IS A HEBREW WORD DEPICTING A
COMPETITIVE RELATIONSHIP THAT IS UNHEALTHY AND IS A RESULT
OF ONE PERSON BEING VIEWED AS LOWER THAN THE OTHER. IN
THIS INSTANCE, BECAUSE ELKANAH LOVED HANNAH MORE,
PENINNAH INTENTIONALLY IRRITATED HANNAH.

But even when Hannah was being ridiculed, she did something that challenges and inspires me. She took her affliction and pain straight to the Lord.

02   Read 1 Samuel 1:9–11. What words describe how Hannah was feeling?

It's important to take note that Hannah went to the Lord in *honesty*. This is not easy. **Honesty has to be practiced—both with ourselves and God.**

Hannah's pleading reveals how much she trusted God in the midst of uncertainty, especially since there's no evidence in the text of how God was going to respond. That's what makes Hannah so relatable to us. She was an ordinary woman who was stuck in a desperate situation.

03   How does Hannah's example encourage you and challenge you?

Later in 1 Samuel 1, Hannah receives her answered prayer:

"And in due time Hannah conceived and bore a son, and she called his name Samuel, for she said, 'I have asked for him from the LORD'" (1 Samuel 1:20).

04   Pay close attention to those words *"in due time."* Write down why you think the Scriptures include this detail.

It's crucial we pause and address something here.

MANY OF YOU DEEPLY RELATE TO HANNAH'S ANXIETY, STRESS, AND SORROW. READING VERSES LIKE THE ONE ABOVE MIGHT CAUSE YOUR HEART TO SINK, BECAUSE YOUR PRAYERS HAVEN'T BEEN ANSWERED.

But, friend, with great tenderness, I want to bear witness to your pain today and say that whatever you are believing God for, I am believing for it *with you.* God hears you and sees you and is moved by your tears. The miracle He offers us doesn't always bring us the answers we so desperately want, but God promises to remain near to us and to continue working in us.

AND THAT IS STILL A MIRACLE. IT JUST MAY NOT BE THE ONE YOU'VE BEEN EXPECTING.

READ 1 SAMUEL 2:1–10. HERE WE FIND ONE OF THE MOST BEAUTIFUL
SONGS OF WORSHIP AND PRAISE IN THE OLD TESTAMENT.

HANNAH'S RESPONSE IS FRAMED IN THREE IMPORTANT WAYS:
HER HEART, HORN, AND MOUTH (1 SAMUEL 2:1).

Hannah's Response

. . . MY *HEART* EXULTS IN THE LORD; *v. 1a, emphasis added*

For the ancient Israelites:

- the heart was the wellspring of emotion and volition.
- the heart expressed feelings and desires.
- the heart was the seat of the will.

Our hearts pump out love, and what we love we look to.
All of Hannah's sorrow and despair were channeled
into a God-exulting prayer.

. . . MY *HORN* IS EXALTED IN THE LORD *v. 1a, emphasis added*

- Referencing a bull's horn used like a trumpet, a megaphone, a flask for oil.
- Ancient Near East, the metaphor of a wild bull was used to symbolize strength and victory.[11]

In Hannah's prayer, scholars say the horn imagery communicates
God-given strength and dignity.[12]

. . . MY *MOUTH* DERIDES MY ENEMIES, BECAUSE I REJOICE IN YOUR SALVATION. *v. 1b, emphasis added*

From our mouths comes the opportunity:

- to bless or curse.
- to praise or plead.
- to ask questions or cast judgment.

Hannah used her mouth to reflect what was true within her heart
and in her raised horn she proclaimed the defeat of her enemies.[13]

05   Using Biblegateway.com or Biblehub.com, read 1 Samuel 2:1b and write down how these translations describe the action of *the mouth:*

ESV

NASB

NIV

NLT

CSB

Pro tip:

WHENEVER YOU NOTICE THAT THERE ARE DIFFERENT ENGLISH WORDS USED IN DIFFERENT TRANSLATIONS OF THE BIBLE, THIS IS A GOOD INDICATION THAT A BIBLE WORD STUDY WOULD BE HELPFUL. DIFFERENT ENGLISH TRANSLATIONS CAN MEAN THE TRANSLATORS WERE WORKING HARD TO BRING CLARITY TO A WORD NOT EASILY TRANSLATED INTO ENGLISH.

All of the translations share a common idea: The mouth speaks out against the enemy and proclaims victory because of the salvation the Lord brings.

In 1 Samuel 2:9, when Hannah says *"my enemies"* she does not make an attack against her personal enemy but remembers that something bigger is going on beyond just her situation. Hannah speaks out against the enemies of God.

It's easy to blame or attack people who are compounding hurt in a hard situation or seem to be the root of a problem. But, friend, what would happen if we stepped back and remembered the ongoing, bigger conflict between God and His enemies?

06   Read Ephesians 6:10–20. What do these verses tell us about the bigger conflict that is happening?

The Lord, in His kindness, never leaves us to battle alone. In fact, the reason we can lift our "horns" and proclaim from our mouths with joyful hearts is because of God and the promise of the Messiah. Look at 1 Samuel 2:10 to find the evidence of the prophecy we want to leave you with today:

"The adversaries of the LORD shall be broken to pieces; against them he will thunder in heaven. The LORD will judge the ends of the earth; he will give strength to his king and exalt the horn of his anointed" (emphasis added).

The identity of the king can be found in the Hebrew word translated as *"anointed"*: *mashiakh*, מָשִׁיחַ. This is the Messiah! Hannah is not speaking of some future, human king; she is prophesying of the *King of kings*, Jesus![14]

What an incredible and important moment.

THOUSANDS OF YEARS BEFORE JESUS WOULD BE BORN IN BETHLEHEM, HANNAH'S PROPHETIC SONG HAD KING JESUS IN MIND. HANNAH'S LONGING AND WAITING LED TO THE BIRTH OF HER OWN SON, AND SHE ALSO FORETOLD GOD'S ONE AND ONLY SON WHO WOULD EVENTUALLY COME TO EARTH.

Poetry

———

For the Lord declared, "I have placed my chosen king on the throne in Jerusalem, on my holy mountain."

PSALM 2:6 NLT

The Old Testament includes A LOT of different kings which can be confusing. We even saw evidence of kingship in Hannah's story yesterday. Not only are there a lot of kings to keep straight, but there are also historical references that might feel unfamiliar to us in our culture today. But that's why we're going through this study together!

Today we find ourselves in Psalm 2. The heading of Psalm 2 in the ESV translation says "The Reign of the Lord's Anointed" and in the CSB translation it says "Coronation of the Son."

Psalm 2 is often referred to as a "coronation psalm" or a "royal psalm," and it's actually one of the most quoted psalms in the New Testament, referenced at least 19 times. Let's talk about what happens during one of these "crowning ceremonies" and how people would have felt about it.

The coronation of the new king came with all the "ideals" this new kingship promised. A new king could bring better security, power, wealth, and opportunity that may have been lacking in the previous king. This was important because most of the kings during this time were found untrustworthy and didn't live up to the king the people longed for.

This is why having an "ideal" other than God can be such a slippery slope. It's so very easy for these "ideals" to lead to large frustrations and ultimately letdowns because things and people will inevitably fail us.

01   Read Psalm 2:1–3. What are the kings of the nations doing?

02   Continue reading Psalm 2:4–5 in the CSB translation. What is the response of the *"one enthroned"*?

We see revealed, right in the middle of the text, a prophetic song of a different kind of King. Not an untrustworthy, earthly king who would fail the people of Israel but an ever-faithful, eternal King who would soon save all people: King Jesus.

If you recall in our study of Hannah yesterday, we learned the Hebrew word *mashiakh* ,מָשִׁיחַ, translated as "anointed," is also the word for "Messiah."

03   Go back and read Psalm 2:2. What word do you see again?

Yep, it's the same word. This psalmist is not just talking about an ideal human king but rather the expectation for the *"Anointed"* Son (Psalm 2:2) who is the King set on Mount Zion (Psalm 2:6). The ESV Bible translation says He is *"begotten"* of the King, and He is enthroned in the heavens (Psalm 2:7b). This royal coronation song of Psalm 2 is a prophetic song of anticipation for the real King of kings: the Anointed One, none other than King Jesus.

Because King Jesus is the ideal King, He can live up to the ideal standards no human king ever could. We can trust Him like no other leader because He will care for us and lead us like no other leader.

04   What characteristics of Jesus make Him the ideal leader? Which of the characteristics you listed would you personally like to grow in?

MOUNT ZION IS AN IMPORTANT LOCATION MENTIONED OFTEN THROUGHOUT THE OLD TESTAMENT.

Mount Zion is often referred to as and believed to be the place where God dwells and rules (see Isaiah 8:18). Sometimes, the temple is referred to as "Zion" or "Mt. Zion" or "the holy hill" because, again, the temple is where God would dwell (see Psalm 76:1–2). Zion is also sometimes referred to as the city that is on top of the mountain, that would be the future hope of the people of God and the place where God would rule and reign over the world (Micah 4:7).

Let's look a little deeper into how this prophecy becomes even more real through specific examples of the life of Jesus.

- One of the central themes of all of Scripture is not just kings or kingship but the Kingdom of God.[15] In the Old Testament, there is a constant picture of God as King. In the New Testament, Jesus' primary message, especially in the teachings of the Gospels, is the arrival of the "kingdom of God" because the King, Christ, entered human history by coming to earth and dwelling among us (Mark 1:14–15).
- This coronation psalm would actually have been sung or stated through multiple celebrations on a single day. But the coronation of Jesus took place repeatedly throughout His earthly ministry as the "Sonship" of Jesus was affirmed multiple times. God the Father addressed Jesus as "my son," and that's why Jesus is often referred to as the "Son of God."

As we learned last week, most of the ancient kings of Israel were a disappointment. They couldn't live up to the "ideal" king the people longed for because they were human. The "ideal" king was prophesied to us through the royal coronation song of Psalm 2. We now have the very best King in Jesus.

Jesus "inherited" (reclaimed) the nations by His spilled blood on the cross, tearing down the dividing wall of hostility (Ephesians 2) and making those who were once enemies into brothers and sisters. He created reconciliation in a way that no earthly king could accomplish.

Jesus conquered the enemies of God, by conquering sin, the devil and ultimately death through His own death, burial, resurrection, and ascension.

The people of Israel longed for *rescue*, but what they really needed was *redemption*.

Redemption is the ultimate rescue because it grants us something we could never obtain on our own: freedom from sin and death. And only King Jesus could grant us this gift of redemption by conquering death sacrificing His own life.

Friend, whatever or whomever you may be looking to for rescue today, invite Jesus into that space right now. Colossians 1:13 says, *"He has delivered us from the domain of darkness and transferred us to the kingdom of his beloved Son."* Even when we aren't rescued from going through difficult circumstances, because of Jesus, redemption is always possible. His redemption means that evil will not have the final say in your story or mine.

As we continue to see Jesus throughout the Bible, I pray you not only begin to see Jesus in unexpected ways in your life right now but also see His love for you revealed from the very beginning of time.

Minor Prophets

MICAH 5 / JOHN 10:22–42

But you, O Bethlehem Ephrathah, who are too little to be among the clans of Judah, from you shall come forth for me one who is to be ruler in Israel, whose coming forth is from of old, from ancient days.

MICAH 5:2

As we have studied different prophecies of Jesus this week, remember there are also sections in the Old Testament called "the Prophets." These books are often split into the Minor Prophets and the Major Prophets. This isn't based on their importance but their length of content. Today we are going to look into the book of Micah, one of the Minor Prophets.

Let's start by reading Micah 5:1–6, which is sometimes referred to as an "oracle," or an announcement of hope regarding a future ruler. However, at this point in history, the audience would have had a long history of failure by their kings. Plus, the Israelites found themselves once again between a hard place (the northern kingdom of Israel had fallen to the Assyrians) and an even harder place (Micah prophesied of their own future judgment). The thought of a ruler over Israel who would finally assure their security seemed too good to be true.

01   What is making you skeptical of God's good promises right now?

As we've previously mentioned, sometimes biblical prophecy has a bifocal nature. In Micah 5:1–6, we see this duality revealed, as Micah first casts a vision for an immediate future but also communicates an echo of what's to come.

Micah 5:1 says, *"Now muster your troops, O daughter of troops; siege is laid against us; with a rod they strike the judge of Israel on the cheek."* Let's discuss what is being referenced in this verse:

- The *"siege"* refers to the Babylonian King Nebuchadnezzar and his army who attacked Israel, destroyed Jerusalem and carried Judah into captivity.[16]
- The *"judge of Israel"* would be King Zedekiah, the last "ruler/judge" of Judah and therefore of "Israel."
- The significance of this judge of Israel being *"struck on the cheek"* with a rod could be a reference to any damage or harm that is done to the face. So King Zedekiah was figuratively "struck on the cheek," and in actuality, his eyes were gouged out.
- The *"rod"* comes from the Hebrew word *shēvet* ,שֵׁבֶט and can also be translated as "scepter," which also helps give context to the situation of Micah 5:1.[17] The scepter was a symbol that conveyed leadership, power and dominion. So what we find in Micah 5:1 is that the enemy of Israel would use the full weight of their military power against Israel.

All of these historical details prepare us to learn about another King, very different from King Zedekiah, who would also face attack and suffer in some similar ways.

02   Read Matthew 27:30 and record the details of what's taking place.

03   Read Mark 15:19 and record the details of what's taking place.

04   Read John 19:3 and record the details of what's taking place.

We've already learned how King Jesus is not just better than any Old Testament king, but He is the *ultimate* King. However, while He always reigned with complete sovereignty, He was not spared suffering while on earth. Jesus had enemies just like any king would. He was struck by those with power (remember the "scepter"). And as Jesus was handed over for crucifixion, He was physically struck on the jaw.

This also takes us back to Day 6 this week in Genesis 3:15, where we uncovered that Jesus would be struck by the enemy, but in the end, Jesus would claim forever victory and reclaim His people from the grips of sin and death.

05   How does hearing about the suffering and persecution of Jesus give you even greater insight that He understands the pain we're in when we walk through these things, too?

Micah 5:2

- LOCATION OF THE BIRTH OF THE FUTURE KING
  AS *"BETHLEHEM EPHRATHAH"*
- AT LEAST TWO CITIES NAMED BETHLEHEM
- BETHLEHEM EPHRATHAH WAS NEAR JERUSALEM (JOSHUA 19:15)[18]
- SAME BETHLEHEM AS LEGENDARY KING DAVID'S
  HOMETOWN (SEE 1 SAMUEL 16:1)
- PROPHECY CONNECTS BACK TO THE PROMISE
  GOD MADE TO DAVID THAT SOMEONE FROM HIS
  LINEAGE WOULD ALWAYS BE ON THE THRONE OF ISRAEL
  (2 SAMUEL 7:16)

Micah 5:4

- THIS KING WILL RULE "IN THE MAJESTY OF THE NAME OF THE LORD
  [YAHWEH] HIS GOD"
- CONNECTION TO JESUS THE MESSIAH
- JESUS WAS THE FAITHFUL SON OF GOD, SAME IN ESSENCE AS THE
  FATHER BUT DISTINCT IN PERSON
- OLD TESTAMENT PEOPLE REFERRED TO GOD AS "YAHWEH"
- JESUS COULD LIVE, ACT, AND RULE IN THE NAME OF YAHWEH
  BECAUSE JESUS WAS YAHWEH (JOHN 10:30)

Micah 5:5

- PROMISE OF THIS FUTURE KING IS PEACE
- HUMANITY LONGED FOR PEACE SINCE GENESIS 3

WHAT A BEAUTIFUL MYSTERY TO TRY AND WRAP OUR MINDS AROUND:
JESUS IS GOD AND THEREFORE ALL OF HIS ACTIONS ARE A PERFECT
REFLECTION AND REPRESENTATION OF THE CHARACTER OF GOD
THE FATHER.

Let's look at the description of the peace that the Messiah would bring and how He would bring it. First, Jesus is Peace. But just because Jesus is peace doesn't mean there wasn't chaos, confusion, or conflict that surrounded Him and the disciples. It does mean that Jesus brought the peace in the middle of the circumstances.

Today, we stand in the middle of hope. We know Jesus came and we are waiting for Him to return. So what does this prophecy teach us to do in the meantime? Micah 5:1 tells us: Gather, prepare, and eventually fight back against the siege.

Friend, the people of God are always given something to do while we wait for hope to be made completed. We can gather as the family of God, pray, worship, serve our communities, and share the encouraging Truth of Jesus and aim to be that brilliant light, like a city on a hill, that illuminates the darkness (Matthew 5:16).

Because God is not absent, we are not waiting in hopelessness but in hopeful anticipation.

*for more correlations between Old Testament and New Testament in Micah 5:2-6, see appendix

Messiah

ISAIAH 9:1-7 / MATTHEW 18:1-8

———

For to us a child is born, to us a son is given; and the government shall be upon his shoulder, and his name shall be called Wonderful Counselor, Mighty God, Everlasting Father, Prince of Peace.

ISAIAH 9:6

We started this week talking about how prophecy can include future events that are immediate and others that are further away. Today, we are going to study an Old Testament prophecy that promised the Messiah (Jesus) would not only come, but when He came He would bring justice and righteousness.

It can seem like justice and righteousness are rare in our world today. Even a quick look in our history books shows that every generation has experienced heartache as a result of injustice in our communities, societies, and world. But probably most jarring of all is when we experience injustice personally in our homes, workplaces or even churches.

01   Whether it's something you're aware of from the news or something you've seen up close and personal, what injustice is breaking your heart right now?

When we look back at the Old Testament, we find God has always cared about these issues. God's heart of special care for the oppressed and hurting is evidence of His great compassion and desire to see all people, from all nations, be welcomed into the family of God.

But like any family we must deal with injustice, corruption, and unrighteousness when we become aware of it.

This is why the prophecy of the coming Messiah in Isaiah 9:6–7 includes some important details. The Messiah would bring with Him what was needed to deal with the hurt of the world.

6 "For to us a child is born,
to us a son is given;
and the government shall be upon his shoulder,
and his name shall be called
Wonderful Counselor, Mighty God,
Everlasting Father, Prince of Peace.
7 Of the increase of his government and of peace
there will be no end,
on the throne of David and over his kingdom,
to establish it and to uphold it
with justice and with righteousness
from this time forth and forevermore.
The zeal of the LORD of hosts will do this."

It's common to hear Isaiah 9:6 read aloud at Christmas. But sometimes verse 7 gets lost in the focus on verse 6. Keeping these verses together brings more context and power to them both.

Let's define two terms found in verse 7 so we have a common understanding of our foundation before diving in further. Those words are "justice" and "righteousness."

Justice

COMES FROM THE HEBREW WORD
"MISHPAT" AND REFERS TO A
LEGAL DECISION.

OLD TESTAMENT STANDARD:
THE LAW

Righteousness

COMES FROM THE HEBREW WORD
"TSEDEQ," MEANING RIGHTNESS
BASED ON A STANDARD.[19]

NEW TESTAMENT STANDARD:
JESUS AS FULFILLMENT
OF THE LAW

We see justice and righteousness fleshed out in two significant ways throughout the Old Testament:[20]

GOD IS JUST AS HE FULFILLS THE
SALVATION HE HAS PROMISED IN
THE OLD TESTAMENT, THROUGH
THE MESSIAH WHOM THE NEW
TESTAMENT DECLARES IS JESUS.

GOD IN HIS RIGHTEOUSNESS
RESPONDS TO THE OPPRESSION
OF THOSE WHO ARE IN
AFFLICTION.

With these definitions and examples in mind, we can now see what Isaiah 9:6–7 prophesies about the Messiah. These verses tell us a lot about Jesus.

It's also important to focus on the names associated with Jesus.

02   Go back to Isaiah 9:6. List the words used to describe the names of this *"son."*

This verse translated in English gives us four phrases as a description: *"Wonderful Counselor, Mighty God, Everlasting Father, Prince of Peace"* (Isaiah 9:6).[21]

However, in Hebrew, we should really only see two thoughts written as a sentence:

Wonderful Counselor, Mighty God   AND   **Everlasting Father, Prince of Peace**

03   Which of these names means the most to you right now and why?

Let's take a deeper look at these two phrases:

Wonderful Counselor, Mighty God

The phrase combines two important thoughts. First, that Jesus is wonderful. But what is He wonderful at? The word "counselor" deals with planning and strategy. In the Hebrew language it has overtones of military planning. Think of a brilliant military general who makes plans and gives wise counsel. He is mighty to act out and accomplish everything that He plans.

Everlasting Father, Prince of Peace

This phrase suggests that the Messiah (Jesus) is the *"Everlasting Father,"* a striking claim that affirms His divine nature. The Father is also a *"Prince,"* who brings about shalom.

How will this all come about? Through the Messiah as He rules through justice and righteousness.

Let's finish today by looking at some verses about how we can do this:

04   Read Matthew 5:6 and Matthew 6:33. What stands out to you?

05   Go to the book of James and look at the following verses: James 1:9–10; 2:1–10; 5:1–6. Meditate on the verses that stand out to you and jot down some personal takeaways.

AS WE CLOSE THIS WEEK'S STUDY,
LET'S PRAY TOGETHER.

Father God, thank You for the truths we
unpacked this week in Your Word. I praise You
for these revelations You are showing me while
I find myself in my own waiting place. I pray
right now that You would strengthen my faith
today. Show me more of You. And thank You
for Your Son, Jesus. He is evidence that reminds me
You always keep Your promises. Continue to show
me more of Him in the coming weeks of this study.
In Jesus' Name, Amen.

Patterns

Welcome to Week 3, friend.

This week, we are diving into how we can see Jesus throughout the Bible in patterns.

Patterns are everywhere in Scripture, but in the Old Testament particularly, the earliest patterns are found in Genesis 1–3. Though we've already studied Adam and Eve and the Garden of Eden during this study, we haven't yet focused on the pattern of God and the pattern of the enemy.

Let's first look at the pattern of God from the creation story (Genesis 1–2):

- God plants a **beautiful** garden . . .
- God fills up that garden with **beautiful** things . . .
- God creates the most **beautiful** and unique creation of all, humanity.

God **creates**. What God **creates is good** and beautiful. And God appoints **His good creation** to multiply and fill the earth with evidence of His goodness and glory (Genesis 1:28b). The pattern here is that anything God creates is beautiful and such a brilliant reflection of Himself.

This brings us to the pattern of the serpent, who we know is our enemy, Satan. The enemy's pattern is to separate people from God, from God's beautiful and best plans, and from their fellow humans. As a matter of fact, Satan's name in Hebrew means to oppose, obstruct, or accuse. The Greek word literally means "adversary."[22] So that's his pattern. He creates opposition, obstruction, and accusation all in order to turn us into adversaries. Remember, on Day 3 and Day 6 of this study we've already looked at John 10:10, which shows the extreme measures Satan will take to separate us from God and from one another: He will steal, kill, and destroy.

The serpent tempts Adam and Eve to go against God's instructions by enticing them to think that if they eat from the tree of the knowledge of good and evil, they won't die but instead *"will be like God"* (Genesis 3:5). The irony and tragedy of this story is that God had already made Adam and Eve in His image. They were already like God.

Don't miss this. *They were already like God*. And when they took the bait of the enemy, he lured them away from being like God. So, in sinning, Adam and Eve got the exact opposite of the outcome they had hoped for. God's plan for good was not only interrupted, but separation between God and His creation was present for the very first time.

God's pattern is to bring about good.

The enemy's pattern is to bring about evil.

The pattern of humans is wanting good but continuing to sin, which disrupts God's plan for good.

Despite the human pattern of sin, God doesn't pivot His plans for good. God doesn't leave things broken. Even though separation was created, it would not be permanent.

God would send a Rescuer. And though the heel of this promised Rescuer would be bruised, eventually, the head of the enemy would be crushed. (See Genesis 3:15 or Week 2, Day 6 of this study.)

How incredible is that? Though God's original pattern was interrupted by sin, God set a new pattern into motion.

- God promises good to humanity . . .
- Humanity responds with rebellion and breaks relationship with God . . .
- God promises that the relationship will not be broken

forever, but the path to reunion will include pain . . .
- Jesus endures this pain, conquers evil, pays the price for humanity's sin, and restores the possibility of a relationship between God and humanity.

So, with Jesus, the pattern we see is one of *redemptive reversals*. Jesus is the redeemer of all things. But we can especially see this in His reversing the effects of sin and starting the process of redemption, even in the Old Testament, by restoring mankind back to God's best. Be sure to put some thought into the questions this week so you can see how the pattern of humans turning away from God, since the beginning of time, is often repeated in our lives as well.

But the great news is that Jesus' pattern to redeem and reverse has been evident throughout history and is very much still active in our lives, too. This week, we will look for Jesus as we study the patterns of famine and rain, falling and rising, wilderness and promised land, less-than and greater-than, and chaos and order.

Jesus is the hope of these redemptive reversals and the new pattern God the Father put into motion. We will see the hope in what's harsh, the new life in what's nearly dead, and the possibilities in what may look impossible.

Our redeemer lived. Our redeemer lives. Nothing is beyond His ability to reverse. What a great comfort that is!

Famine and Rain

AMOS 8 / JOHN 7:37–43

———

O God, you are my God; earnestly I seek you; my soul thirsts for you;
my flesh faints for you, as in a dry and weary land where there is no water.

PSALM 63:1

Do you ever look around at all that is happening in our world today and feel fear grip your heart?

We crave safety and certainty and simplicity as we raise our families, serve God and live out our Christian beliefs. But so many things feel threatening to those desires, and fear can seem so consuming.

01   What are you afraid of right now?

The number-one thing the Israelites feared most was *famine*. They were primarily farmers, and their livelihood depended on rainfall to produce crops. Insufficient rain led to famine, and famine meant sure death.

02   What do the following verses also teach us about the importance of rain?

LEVITICUS 26:4

DEUTERONOMY 28:12

EZEKIEL 34:26

The pattern of rain and famine was this: Where there was rain, there was a fear that famine would return. Where there was famine, there was a desperation for rain.

You may not fear a lack of rain, but we all know fear. And when fear begins to consume us, we reach for anything to help us regain a sense of control. We can see this clearly in how the Israelites began to react.

Only God could provide rain or keep rain back from them. This is why the Israelites may have been tempted to worship and follow Baal, the Canaanite thunder/storm god. They couldn't control God so they stopped trusting Him.

03   Let that last sentence sit with you for just a minute. Is there a part of you that can relate to the Israelites here?

The Israelites were so afraid of famine, and lacked trust that God would provide, that they copied the pagans around them and started worshipping and sacrificing to false gods that represented weather, rain, fertility, and more. God had made it very clear to the Israelites that they were to have no other gods besides Him (Exodus 20:3), but in trying to control their fears and vulnerabilities, they disobeyed.

04   Read Jeremiah 3:2–3 and Amos 4:7–8. Why did God withhold rain in these verses?

IN AN EFFORT TO PREVENT A FAMINE, THE ISRAELITES WOUND UP CAUSING ONE.

They refused to recognize that turning away from God was the same as choosing to turn toward sin.

And the drought in their spiritual lives led to a drought in their physical lives. This is where we see the redemption of Jesus. He takes humanity's deep physical desire for water and uses it to reveal an even more crucial soul-need for Living Water. Then He doesn't just reveal our need—He becomes the conduit through which the redemptive Living Water of God comes to us.

Now that we've seen how this fear of famine played out in a nation of people, let's see how it played out with an individual. To do that, we'll take another look at the life of King David.

05   Read Psalm 63:1. What connection do you see between famine and rain in the words of the psalmist, King David?

David compares his deep desire for God to a persistent thirst. David's thirst is attributed to *"a dry and weary land where there is no water,"* which is another way of describing a famine (Psalm 63:1). David knew the ache of physical thirst and longing. But David also knew the deep ache of spiritual thirst.

Maybe, like David, you're facing a situation you can't change no matter what you do . . . and you're still left *thirsty*.

If you're in this place, you're not alone. In fact, you're poised to have a real encounter with Jesus. Where you feel empty is an exact appointment to experience true Living Water. In fact, Jesus Himself tells us this.

John 7:37–38 says, *"On the last day of the feast, the great day, Jesus stood up and cried out, 'If anyone thirsts, let him come to me and drink. Whoever believes in me, as the Scripture has said, "Out of his heart will flow rivers of living water."'"*

Jesus even says in John 4:14 that *". . . whoever drinks of the water that I will give him will never be thirsty again. The water that I will give him will become in him a spring of water welling up to eternal life."*

WHAT WE'RE REALLY THIRSTING FOR IS THE LIVING WATER THAT JESUS BRINGS.

Amos 8:11–12 spoke to this thirst. Many people are emotionally and spiritually dying of soul starvation because they need the Word of God. They may have physical access to God's Word, but there's a big difference between physical access and personal access. Just because most of our homes probably have a couple of Bibles in them doesn't mean we are personally accessing the Scriptures and nourishing our souls.

But instead of going to God and turning to His Word, sometimes we try to seek satisfaction from solutions of our own making. We keep trying to quench that deep-soul thirst with people, possessions, positions, and platforms. While some of these things can fill us for a season, they eventually leave us desperately empty and thirsty. Only Jesus can quench the deep longings of our soul.

Oh, friends. Our souls are tailor-made to be filled with Jesus and His Truth. That means nothing else will be able to refresh, restore, and transform us. Nothing else will ever truly satisfy our souls. None of those solutions or idols we reach for in a desperate need for control will bring us lasting satisfaction and peace.

All of these verses from the Old and New Testaments are coming together to remind us that our souls have a real hunger and thirst that God created in us. And every longing is a reminder for us to look to Jesus as the only real way to access God's Living Water.

AND LIKE JESUS PREACHES IN MATTHEW 5:6,

"Blessed are those who hunger and thirst for righteousness, for they will be filled" (NIV).

Various Famines in the Bible

PATRIARCHAL PERIOD (GENESIS 12:10; GENESIS 26:1)	Abraham and Isaac migrate to escape famine. Where do they go? Egypt. Here we see a pattern: As a result of the seven-year famine, Jacob and his family live in . . . EGYPT (Genesis 41:57; Genesis 45:5–7; compare Acts 7:11)!
PRE-MONARCHIC (BEFORE KINGS)	Ruth and Elimilech migrate to Moab because of famine (Ruth 1:1).
MONARCHIC (TIME OF THE KINGS)	Elijah, on behalf of God, initiates a three-year famine in the time of King Ahab. (1 Kings 17:1; 1 Kings 18:1–2; compare Luke 4:25) There is also a seven-year famine during the lifetime of Elisha (2 Kings 4:38; 2 Kings 8:1).
POSTEXILIC (AFTER THE EXILE)	Haggai talks about a famine during the time of the Persians (Haggai 1:10–11; 2:16). Nehemiah 5 records a famine.
NEW TESTAMENT	In Acts, Agabus prophesies of a famine that most likely took place during the time of the emperor Claudius (AD 41–54) and is referred to in extra-biblical sources (Tacitus, *Annals* 12.43).

Rising and Falling

GENESIS 37 / PHILIPPIANS 2:5–11

And we know that for those who love God all things work together for good,
for those who are called according to his purpose.

ROMANS 8:28

Have you ever cried over something so much that you felt like you'd run out of tears? Your eyes are swollen while a current of unrest still rages through your soul. And you look up toward heaven in utter confusion . . . "God, why aren't You doing something?"

Why aren't You answering my prayer?
Why aren't You intervening in this hopeless situation?
Why are You allowing this to happen?
Why, God?

This is the crux of one of the hardest parts about following God . . . You know He is all-powerful and can literally do anything, but it's devastating when He is not demonstrating His power through the things you are begging Him for most.

01   How do you resonate with these questions and feelings in your life right now?

Unanswered prayers can leave us feeling like we keep hitting a detour instead of our intended destination. Detours that go on for too long can begin to feel more like dead ends. What we thought was a pause turns into a screeching halt.

The story of Joseph is one with detours and what seemed like dead ends. We encounter his story starting in Genesis 37. There are many parts of Joseph's story that felt less like a detour and more like an actual reversal of the direction he thought his life would go . . . There were long stretches of time when it must have felt like God was doing nothing.

And we might have similar feelings when we've hit a dead end and nothing looks like we expected:

THAT PRAYER WILL NEVER BE ANSWERED . . .

THE RELATIONSHIP WE'VE DREAMED OF WILL NEVER BE REALITY . . .

THE DREAM OF DOING MINISTRY WILL NEVER HAPPEN . . .

THE PAIN WILL NEVER GO AWAY . . .

THE HEALING WON'T BE POSSIBLE . . .

THE FALSE ACCUSATIONS AGAINST US WILL NEVER BE RIGHTED . . .

THE HARD CIRCUMSTANCES WILL NEVER GET BETTER . . .

02   If you find yourself in what feels like a dead end, what are some of the lies you're tempted to believe? Confess some of these and open your heart to what God may want to show you today.

Joseph's journey shows us that God is still with us even when we feel like we are falling behind, stuck in detours, and derailed from our ideal plan. Joseph's story also shows that even when we fall, we will eventually rise. Detours and dead ends may be a part of our story, but they're never the *whole* story.

JOSEPH HAD TIMES WHERE HE TEMPORARILY FELL BACK INTO
WHAT FELT LIKE A DETOUR, BUT THEN HE EVENTUALLY ROSE.

Here, we see a pattern of rising and falling. Let's take a look at some of these events:

Joseph has a dream that his family will bow down to him.

Joseph is stripped of his clothes and thrown into a pit.

Joseph is sold into slavery but finds a position of honor in Potiphar's house.

Joseph acts with integrity and honor and refuses the sexual advances of Potiphar's wife, but this refusal lands him in prison.

Joseph gains leadership opportunities and even becomes friends with the cupbearer and baker in the prison, where he later interprets their dreams. As a result, Joseph is later called upon to interpret Pharaoh's dreams and is exalted into a position of high honor, second in power only to Pharaoh himself.

How could you be thrown into a pit by your family, sold into slavery, and then unfairly imprisoned without looking at God and asking "Why?" Joseph's *falls* were not just little bumps in the road. And the *rising* moments did not feel like instant relief. No, there were stretches of time in between these rising and falling events.

God had a plan. And his brothers' betrayal was not the end of Joseph's story. From the pit to the palace, Joseph was eventually positioned to spare the lives of his family and the entire nation of Israel.

03   Reflect on some of the details of Joseph's story. What stands out to you the most?

This rising and falling pattern doesn't just apply to Joseph. We actually see the same pattern revealed in Jesus' life.

FALLING — Jesus condescends* onto earth.

RISING — Jesus is baptized and affirmed by God the Father.

FALLING — Jesus is led by the Spirit into the wilderness.

RISING — Jesus enters the city of Jerusalem in His triumphal entry.

FALLING — Jesus embarks on the journey to the cross and crucifixion.

RISING — Jesus rises from the grave, conquering sin and death on the third day.

* "Condescension" is a theological term that refers to the incarnation of Christ, specifically that Christ "came down" from heaven onto the earth. The emphasis is placed on the "coming down." So when we mention "falling," this is to highlight moments where God "stooped" for us, in love. "Rising," on the other hand, highlights clear moments of victory.

Even during our "falling" times, God is still working. How did God use the times when Jesus "fell"? How has God used some of your "falling" times?

The tension between the falling and rising can often create what look like detours and dead ends. But through the examples of Joseph and Jesus, we see another redemptive reversal: Good is where God leads us. Even when what we're experiencing right now doesn't feel good, we can trust that, no matter what, God never derails from His plan of eventual good . . . in His way, in His timing.

There may be situations, circumstances, diagnoses, and outcomes that don't seem good in the moment, but God's story for us never stops at a dead end. Romans 8:28 reminds us of this: *"And we know that for those who love God all things work together for good, for those who are called according to his purpose."*

And we pray, as you reflect further on the evidence of this in Scripture, you are even more encouraged by how faithful God is to us. He was working for good in the suffering of Joseph. He was working for good in the suffering of Jesus. And the same is true for us. But even better because we have the assurance of the ultimate good Jesus made a way for us to experience in eternity.

This leads us to another pattern we will study next: the in-between places of our lives that look like wilderness experiences. Tomorrow we will study the wilderness and promised land.

Wilderness and Promised Land

DEUTERONOMY 32:10–11 / MATTHEW 4:1–11

———

*He humbled you, causing you to hunger and then feeding you with manna, which neither you
nor your ancestors had known, to teach you that man does not live on bread alone
but on every word that comes from the mouth of the LORD.*

DEUTERONOMY 8:3

Earlier, in Week 1, we looked into the lives of Moses and Joshua. During that study, we touched on the Israelites' journey from the wilderness to the promised land. This journey also represents a deeper pattern we can trace to Jesus.

Throughout the Old Testament, the people of God found themselves in perpetual cycles of wilderness or desert experiences, with small glimpses of what the promised land would be like.

There are multiple Hebrew words *midbar, yeshimōn, tōhu* that translate into "desert," "wilderness," or "wasteland."[23] In fact, Genesis 1:2 says, *"The earth was without form* [tōhu] *and void . . ."* showing us the very first picture of this concept. The world was a wilderness or wasteland before God began creating the beauty of Eden and eventually His image bearers, Adam and Eve.

There is the physical experience of a wilderness, but there's also a spiritual experience.

A SPIRITUAL WILDERNESS CAN *FEEL LIKE* THE ABSENCE OF GOD.

It is feeling alone and hidden in suffering for an extended period of time. You know God is there, but you don't feel Him at all.

01   Can you recall a time when you felt this way? What situation felt like a wilderness season to you?

Conversely, the promised land is marked by evidence of the **presence of God.** This was an actual place the Israelites ventured. For us, it spiritually symbolizes the fruitfulness of God. Maybe we have received answered prayers, breakthroughs in situations, or even a season of close intimacy with God. It's a time when you hear Him more clearly than you have before.

02   Can you recall a time when God felt close? What was happening in your life? What did you learn?

THE EARTH IS VOID, DARK AND FILLED WITH CHAOS. (GENESIS 1:1–2) → **WILDERNESS**

GOD PLANTS A BEAUTIFUL GARDEN AND PLACES ADAM AND EVE IN THE GARDEN TO CARE FOR, KEEP AND TEND TO IT. (GENESIS 2:15) — **PROMISED LAND**

ADAM AND EVE ARE CAST OUT OF EDEN. (GENESIS 3:23) — **(WILDERNESS)**

GOD SAVES NOAH AND RE-CREATES THE EARTH TO START OVER. (GENESIS 6–9) — **PROMISED LAND**

THE PEOPLE GATHER IN THE PLAINS OF SHINAR (BABYLON) AND BUILD A TOWER IN REBELLION AGAINST GOD. THEY ARE PUNISHED AND DISPERSED. (GENESIS 11:1–9) → **WILDERNESS**

FROM THE EPICENTER OF REBELLION (UR OF THE CHALDEANS/BABEL), GOD CALLS ABRAHAM AND TAKES HIM TO A NEW LAND. (GENESIS 12:1–9) — **PROMISED LAND**

ABRAHAM'S DESCENDANTS EXPERIENCE FAMINE AND GO TO EGYPT FOR SAFETY. (GENESIS 42) ▷ **FALSE PROMISED LAND > WILDERNESS**

GOD RESCUES THE ISRAELITES OUT OF EGYPT. (EXODUS 12–14) — **PROMISED LAND**

THE ISRAELITES SIN AND END UP WANDERING IN THE WILDERNESS FOR 40 YEARS. (EXODUS 16:35) — **WILDERNESS**

THE ISRAELITES, LED BY JOSHUA, ENTER THE PROMISED LAND. (JOSHUA 3) — **(PROMISED LAND)**

ISRAEL EVENTUALLY BECOMES A UNITED KINGDOM UNDER SAUL AND DAVID. (1 SAMUEL 10; 2 SAMUEL 5:3) — **PROMISED LAND**

AFTER SOLOMON'S REIGN, THE UNITED KINGDOM IS DIVIDED. (1 KINGS 12:16–24) — **WILDERNESS**

EVENTUALLY ISRAEL WILL BE TAKEN OVER BY ASSYRIA, BABYLON AND PERSIA AND SUBJUGATED UNDER OPPRESSIVE ROMAN RULE. (ISAIAH 7:18; 2 CHRONICLES 36:17–21; DANIEL 5:28–31; LUKE 2:1–5) → **WILDERNESS > EXILE**

What might God want to teach us in both the wilderness and promised land?

First, let's review how the wilderness journey began for the Israelites. Because of a famine, Jacob and his sons fled to Egypt and lived with Joseph. Egypt held the promise of prosperity, protection, and provision, but in a terrible irony, it became the Israelites' prison. Years later, the Israelites were perceived as a threat and forced into slavery.

Pharaoh finally released the Israelites from their enslavement, but look where they're sent next in Exodus 13:17–18: *"When Pharaoh let the people go, God did not lead them by way of the land of the Philistines, although that was near. For God said, 'Lest the people change their minds when they see war and return to Egypt.' But God led the people around by the way of the* wilderness *toward the Red Sea"* (emphasis added).

God intentionally took Israel through the wilderness. Friend, even if you are in a wilderness season, be encouraged today that, if God is allowing it, He will use it. The wilderness may be a place marked by desperation, drought, devastation, and desolation, but God does not lead us into anything He won't lead us *through*.

03   Read Deuteronomy 8:1–10. List any mention of wilderness, promised land, and evidence of God's faithful activity:

Now read Deuteronomy 32:10–11.

In this passage, we see God caring for His people in their wilderness experience through three metaphors:

PROTECTOR

The language reflects a protective eagle circling her children, keeping them within view. God doesn't hover or smother but allows His children to live with independence, while He remains close enough to intervene if danger should arrive.

TEACHER

The image of a teacher is reflected by an eagle teaching its babies to fly. Sometimes the mother will push the eaglet out of the nest, letting it fall almost 90 feet. Then the mother swoops down and stabilizes the little bird by placing her wing under the baby for support. Then she repeats this process.[24]

God teaches us in a similar fashion. He gives us freedom to make decisions, but He is always near us to provide guidance if we need it. His teaching leads to our internal growth and trust in Him.

LEADER

God is pictured as a hands-on, caring leader. God does not leave His children to wander aimlessly but shows the right path forward, providing the necessary vision, guidance, and wisdom for the future ahead.

04   Between these three roles, which one are you seeing God fulfill for you most specifically right now?

Let's close today by looking at one more person who knew the desolate places and emotions of the wilderness: Jesus.

- As a child, Jesus had a wilderness type of experience as His family escaped to Egypt in hiding (Matthew 2:13–15).
- Jesus was led into the wilderness by the Spirit (Matthew 4:1) and was tempted.

The Israelites had Moses to be their protector, teacher, and leader through the journey of the wilderness. But with Jesus, we see God *Himself* journeying through the wilderness and coming out on the other side as our protector, teacher, and leader.

Because of Jesus, even though we may be far from our promised land, we can always live with the *promise* that He deeply understands, cares, and will never leave us to figure it out on our own.

JESUS, AND ULTIMATELY THE HOLY SPIRIT, BRIDGES THE GAP
BETWEEN THE WILDERNESS WE'RE EXPERIENCING AND THE
PROMISED LAND WE LONG FOR. JESUS IS GOD'S PROMISE
KEPT TO US THAT, NO MATTER WHAT WE'RE WALKING THROUGH,

He will never be absent, and we will never be alone.

Less-Than and Greater-Than

EXODUS 4:1–17 / MATTHEW 5:1–11 AND 43–48

———

But I say to you, Love your enemies and pray for those who persecute you.

MATTHEW 5:44

Sometimes life's circumstances can bring us to a place of deep pain. Whether its rejection, betrayal, or some other disappointment, I try to remember that God has a unique pattern of taking what makes us feel less-than and using it for great things.

THE OPPOSITE CAN BE TRUE AS WELL.

THOSE THINGS THAT MAKE US SUPERIOR, ARE OFTEN INSIGNIFICANT TO GOD.
IT SEEMS, WITH GOD, SMALL IS BIG, AND BIG IS SMALL.

The cheers of the crowds don't mean much.

The simple conversation where we helped someone means everything.

Hundreds or thousands of people following us on social media isn't the big influence we think it is.

Being kind and gracious to that gal who works at the grocery store means more than we know.

THE WORLD TELLS US TO EXALT OURSELVES AND CLIMB THE LADDER OF SUCCESS.

GOD SAYS TO HUMBLE YOURSELF SO THAT HE CAN BE THE ONE TO LIFT YOU UP. (1 PETER 5:6)

THE WORLD PUSHES US TO LIVE IN DIVISION WITH THOSE DIFFERENT FROM US.

GOD SAYS TO "LOVE YOUR ENEMIES AND PRAY FOR THOSE WHO PERSECUTE YOU." (MATTHEW 5:44)

The Bible is full of God's upside-down principles

THE WORLD SAYS DEATH IS THE END OF THE STORY.

GOD USED THE DEATH OF JESUS TO BRING FORTH LIFE, AND HE PROMISES DEATH WILL NEVER AGAIN HAVE THE FINAL WORD. (ROMANS 6:9–11)

THE WORLD TELLS US HOW TO FIT IN.

GOD EMPOWERS US TO BE SET APART AS DIFFERENCE-MAKERS. (MATTHEW 5:13–16)

THE WORLD YELLS, "LIVE YOUR BEST LIFE NOW!"

GOD SAYS THIS LIFE IS FADING, AND YOUR BEST LIFE IS THE ONE YET TO COME. (JAMES 4:14; 1 PETER 1:3–5)

01 How does this help you consider a different perspective with something you're facing right now?

There are other examples of this upside-down pattern in Scripture, but one we will look at today is the pattern of less-than and greater-than. God consistently uses people society would view as less-than, and He proves to the world, through them, He is in fact greater-than.

We see this pattern most significantly with people who were considered less-than because of a situation they were walking through or a status they lacked:

JACOB WAS CONSIDERED LESS-THAN BECAUSE HE WAS THE YOUNGEST SON, BORN WITHOUT THE PRIVILEGES OF THE BIRTHRIGHT THAT COME WITH BEING THE OLDEST BROTHER.

MOSES FELT LESS-THAN BECAUSE OF HIS TROUBLE WITH PUBLIC SPEAKING.

WOMEN LIKE SARAH AND HANNAH WERE THOUGHT OF AS LESS-THAN BECAUSE THEY STRUGGLED WITH BARRENNESS.

DAVID WAS CONSIDERED LESS-THAN BECAUSE HE WAS THE YOUNGEST SON AND WAS LEFT TO TEND THE FLOCKS WHILE HIS OLDER BROTHERS WERE PRESENTED AS THE POTENTIAL FUTURE KINGS OF ISRAEL.

PROPHETS OF THE OLD TESTAMENT LIKE ELIJAH, ELISHA, AMOS, HABAKKUK, AND SO MANY OTHERS WERE TASKED WITH THE RESPONSIBILITY OF GIVING GOD'S WORD TO GOD'S PEOPLE, ONLY TO BE REJECTED AND SHUNNED.

02   Have you ever felt less-than because of a situation or status in your own life? How has this affected you?

During Week 2, we looked at Micah 5:2. Let's look again to see something else about Bethlehem:

"But you, O Bethlehem Ephrathah,
    who are too little *to be among the clans of Judah,*
from you shall come forth for me
    one who is to be ruler in Israel,
whose coming forth is from of old,
    from ancient days" (emphasis added).

The Hebrew word describing Bethlehem as *"little"* is *tsa'ir.* It can mean small, younger, or insignificant.[25] In fact, this is the same word used to describe a younger sibling (Genesis 19:31; Genesis 29:26; Joshua 9:26).[26]

We may be tempted to overlook some of our less-than moments because culture values the opposite. That's when it's important for us to remember Jesus' experience.

He came from a little, insignificant town called Bethlehem (Matthew 2:1; Micah 5:2).

Jesus was born in the shadow of scandal, to a mother who conceived before marriage (Luke 2:4–6).

Jesus was born into a lineage with some unexpected ancestors, including an adulterer and a prostitute (Matthew 1:1–16).
Jesus was raised in Nazareth (John 1:46).
Jesus was likely ordinary-looking (Isaiah 53:2).
Jesus chose fishermen and tax collectors as His disciples (Matthew 4:18–22).
Jesus ate and hung out with the social outcasts of the time. For example:
- A leper (Luke 5:12–16)
- A paralytic (Luke 5:17–26)
- A tax collector (Luke 5:27–32)
- A woman who was caught up in sin, and men caught up in hypocrisy[27] (John 8:1–11)
- A person afflicted with spiritual (demonic) torment (Luke 8:26–39)

Jesus was considered *less-than,* lowly, and therefore unlikely to be the long-awaited Son of God. His own people, the Jews, doubted He was the Messiah!

03   Go to Mark 6:3. What does it say about people's response to who Jesus was?

Why would God choose to reveal His greater-than power through these less-than realities both in the life of people in the Old Testament and in the life of Jesus?

Read 1 Corinthians 1:26–31.
- **This greater-than/less-than pattern reminds us there is nothing outside of God's capability.**

Read Ephesians 2:11– 13.
- **This pattern reveals to us that no one who places their trust in Christ is disqualified in the Kingdom of God.**

Read Matthew 13:31– 32.
- **This pattern challenges us to look for Jesus in seemingly small or insignificant ways.**

04   What connections do you see in all of these Scriptures within the pattern of less-than and greater-than?

God is in the business of bringing great things to life from less-than situations. Miraculous things from the mundane. Powerful things from what looks like weakness. Redeemed things from what seemed like nothing but a loss. God sending Jesus in the circumstances and way He did is only one example of pure evidence of this.

And for us, what if the next big step God wants us to take actually appears small by the world's standards? What if His *great* next step for us looks a little like less-than?

Going the extra mile for someone who can't repay us . . .
Staying when we would prefer to leave . . .
Giving our all to something we want to quit . . .

Sometimes God is inviting us to be a part of great things He is doing, but we may miss the invitation because of its appearance of smallness or insignificance. We'll never know what that next step is if we don't *"listen for GOD's voice in everything [we] do, everywhere [we] go"* Proverbs 3:6 (MSG).

05   To close today, pray about what your small step of obedience may be. How do the less-than moments and attributes of Jesus' life challenge you?

Chaos and Order

GENESIS 4 / JOHN 1:1–18

———

The wolf shall dwell with the lamb, and the leopard shall lie down with the young goat,
and the calf and the lion and the fattened calf together; and a little child shall lead them.

ISAIAH 11:6

Every circle of friends has "the party-planning friend."

They're usually the friend who keeps everyone together, who always has the details straight for celebrations, trips, and more. Some of their friends operate just fine with chaos, but not them. And in the end, everyone around them benefits from their intentionality.

Interestingly enough, there's a pattern in Scripture that looks a lot like this: the pattern of chaos and order. God consistently brings order to disordered situations. His faithfulness continues to bring unity even when sin causes chaos. We can trace this pattern all the way to Jesus.

This is actually the *first pattern* we see in Scripture.

01 Read Genesis 1:1–2. What words are used to describe the state of the world at this point in creation?

All of these descriptions are indicators of chaos. To Old Testament authors, topics like darkness and the sea were consistent images of chaos, disorder, disunity, and destruction. However, we know God didn't leave the world in its original state. In the middle of chaos, God brought order through creation. And interestingly enough, He did so by separating or dividing.

02 Read Genesis 1:1–18 and underline every time you see the word "separated."

The word "separated" here is the Hebrew word בָּדַל (bāḏăl), which means division.

GOD SEPARATED THE LIGHT FROM THE DARKNESS.

GOD SEPARATED THE WATERS, CREATING HEAVEN.

GOD SEPARATED THE WATER INTO ONE PLACE AND CREATES EARTH/DRY LAND, OR EARTH AND SEAS.

GOD SEPARATED THE LIGHTS/SUN AND STARS.

GOD SEPARATED SEA CREATURES FROM AIR CREATURES.

In each act of division God institutes *divine order.* But because of the events following Genesis 1, rebellion interrupts divine order and there is a division God never intended. This separation, a form of chaos, plays out in two ways:

- Separation between God and man (sin).
- Separation among men (conflict).

All of us have experienced the chaos of *conflict.* The situations may be different, but if you do life with people, you will have conflict. Even though conflict is common, that doesn't make it any easier. And this evidence of conflict can be traced all the way back to the first family of creation.

03   Read Genesis 4:1–8. What was the result of this conflict?

Adam and Eve's descendants continued to populate the earth. And the same command God gave to Adam and Eve in the garden in Genesis 1:28, to *"be fruitful and multiply and fill the earth and subdue it,"* was given to their descendants. But they would not carry out this command as God intended. Over and over the people rebelled.

04   Look at Genesis 11 to read about what took place in the plains of Shinar where the people gathered. Instead of reflecting the goodness and glory of God, what did the people do?

At that time, people believed God met with humanity on mountains. But plains are flat. So they built the Tower of Babel. Besides attempting to make a name for themselves, this tower was their solution for God to come down and meet with them, but it was a manufactured mountain built out of idolatry.[28] Let's take a closer look at some of the events that followed:

Remember, anything we turn to instead of God to satisfy us or to save us is an idol. It's a false god.

CHAOS

The Tower of Babel is a form of rebellion in the plains of Shinar. This rebellion results in the division of humanity by diversifying tongues (languages). (Genesis 11:1–9)

CHAOS

As a result of this punishment, the nations spread out into the world, including the Philistines, Hittites, Egyptians, etc., and are in constant war against God's people of Israel.

ORDER

Different judges like Gideon, Samson, Jephthah, etc. are able to establish temporary order in the midst of the division.

ORDER

The united kingdom is established under Saul and David.

CHAOS

Because of the nations that David conquers, he has blood on his hands and cannot build the temple.

ORDER

Solomon builds the temple.

CHAOS

Solomon's reign of peace ends in household rebellion and the division of the kingdom into the northern and southern kingdoms.

Throughout this pattern of chaos and order, we see a few things taking place. In the presence of chaos, God creates something good from nothing. God's good creation chooses sin which brings chaos into God's order. This requires a holy and just God to execute punishment. But God's mercy and kindness is always present, even in, and arguably especially in, the midst of punishment. God's discipline has a purpose—to bring back eventual order.

God's goal is to establish order: order between man and God (reconciliation) and order among men (peace, unity). What is the evidence of this? Jesus.

This is where we see the redemption of Jesus revealed all through the Bible. Jesus redemptively reverses the division of humanity through His work on the cross—bringing lasting order. Acts 10:35–36 says, *"But in every nation the person who fears him and does what is right is acceptable to him. He sent the message to the Israelites, proclaiming the good news of peace through Jesus Christ—he is Lord of all"* (CSB).

05   Read Isaiah 4:2–6; Isaiah 11:1–9; and Isaiah 55:3–4. Take note of some of these prophecies about Jesus through the lens of chaos and order.

We will continue to experience chaos in our lives today. That is the evidence of our sin-soaked world. However, there are two truths we want to leave you with today to provide perspective in spite of this:

- Jesus closed the separation, caused by sin, between God and humanity by making a relationship with God possible for anyone who places their trust in Him (John 1:12–13; John 14:6; Titus 2:11–14).
- The Holy Spirit empowers us to pursue order in the form of peace and unity (Acts 1:8; Ephesians 3:16). Through this, we are actually invited to participate in the pattern. We may not be able to avoid conflict, but we can pray about what Jesus would have us do in the middle of it.

GOD, THANK YOU FOR CONTINUING
TO REVEAL YOURSELF TO ME
THROUGH SCRIPTURE.

Through everything I continue to study,
I pray I would see more of Jesus and it would
drive me into an even deeper relationship
with Him. I thank You today for
Your everlasting faithfulness. I trust You
through every situation I am facing right now.
In Jesus' Name, Amen.

Provisions

I know what it feels like to beg for God's mighty intervention.

I also know what it feels like after an extended period of time with no change: unheard, alone, and neglected. When I feel like the weight of overwhelming heartbreak is on me at 2 a.m. and I feel utterly alone, my prayers get reduced to tear-filled cries. Often, all I can pray is, "Jesus, I love You, and You love me. Please help me."

When we're in this place, our hearts ache. Our minds race. We might not admit this in Bible study or with our friends, but in quiet moments, alone, we secretly wonder: Where has Jesus gone?

When we fix our eyes on our anticipated or desired outcomes, we can sometimes miss how and when God *is* answering our prayers.

We see this pattern of people missing the evidence of God's care and provision throughout Scripture and, ironically, even in the story of Jesus' life. Jesus was the answer to Israel's long-lifted-up prayers for a Messiah, but so many missed God's faithful reply because Jesus didn't show up like they expected. Jesus wasn't an earthly king who came to give temporary victory over the oppressive Roman government, like the people at the time begged God for. He came to bring everlasting victory by becoming the eternal King who died on a cross to save His people. And Jesus wasn't a king born into a palace. No, our savior had much humbler beginnings.

Luke 2:4 sets the scene for the arrival of Jesus: *"So Joseph also went up from the town of Nazareth in Galilee to Judea, to Bethlehem the town of David, because he belonged to the house and line of David"* (NIV).

From the very start, Jesus' birth in Bethlehem fulfilled God's promise for a Messiah (Micah 5:2). Even the very name of this tiny town—"house of bread"—is a prophetic declaration of future provision. The house of bread was where the Bread of Life was born (John 6:35). Bread is also mentioned in part of the Lord's Prayer in Matthew 6 where Jesus teaches us to pray for *"daily bread"* (v. 11). Jesus would also then go on and model that man does not live by bread alone but by the Word of God.

MICAH 5:2

JOHN 6:35

MATTHEW 6:11

WORD OF GOD

You see, **God's promise of provision through Jesus is available to us today.** Even when we feel abandoned as we wait for answered prayers, Jesus is our Daily Bread. His very birth was marked by provision and He has been our physical and spiritual provision from the beginning of time. We even see a pointing to the salvation of Jesus in Genesis 3. God provided animal skins for Adam and Eve to cover themselves after they sinned and realized they were naked. On that day, it was the blood of a sacrificial animal that was shed to provide a covering. On the cross, Jesus provided the ultimate covering of our sins by giving His own life (Matthew 26:28).

As we study how God provided for His people throughout the Old Testament, all the way to the provision of Jesus Himself coming to earth, we have an opportunity to remember that God always keeps His promises. And when we remember this, that same reassurance will ground us today in our seemingly unanswered prayers and empty places where we're wanting assurance of God's intervention and provision.

After all, Jesus is the best kept promise. Our most complete provision and portion (Psalm 73:26). Our forever reminder that we are not left lost, wandering, or helpless. He is the only lasting, satisfying nourishment and perfect sustenance for every longing in our souls.

Let's dig into Week 4, friend.

GENESIS 3:21   MATTHEW 26:28

God's promise of provision through Jesus is available to us today.

Priests

EXODUS 19 / HEBREWS 2:14–18

———

But you are a chosen race, a royal priesthood, a holy nation, a people for his own possession, that you may
proclaim the excellencies of him who called you out of darkness into his marvelous light.

1 PETER 2:9

As a result of the fall in Genesis 3, there's a progressive feeling in the Old Testament that God grows distant from His people. We go from reading about God walking, talking, and intimately communing with Adam and Eve in the Garden to what feels like a complete silence and absence of His presence in the exilic and postexilic periods of Israelite history. That kind of progressive distance from God can feel confusing and maybe even add to our anxiety about Him. *Will He be there for us?*

This week is all about uncovering examples of how God continually provided for His people, and how those provisions can help us see the ultimate provision of God sending Jesus, a living, breathing example of how to live in a sin-soaked world and still remain faithful. God heard the cries of the people throughout the Old Testament and knew His provision of Jesus would be the ultimate answer.

Friend, when we start to feel God is absent, we must know He always has a bigger plan in the works . . . for even better provision than we know to ask for.

01   Describe a time when you felt like God was distant or silent. In hindsight, can you see His plan?

Even when it appeared God seemed absent to His people, He was working out provision for them. But it wouldn't always look like what they thought or hoped for.

You see, as sin continued to cause separation between man and God, God established a way to care for His people through others: priests, prophets, and kings. These formal positions helped fill the gap of separation and served as vehicles for connection to God. We're going to spend the next three days diving into each of these provisional positions, starting today with priests.

We first see priests appear in Exodus 19:5–6 when the Lord gave Moses specific instructions for the people:

"'Now therefore, if you will indeed obey my voice and keep my covenant, you shall be my treasured possession among all peoples, for all the earth is mine; and you shall be to me a kingdom of priests *and a holy nation.' These are the words that you shall speak to the people of Israel"* (emphasis added).

In a striking statement, God says that all of Israel would function as "priests"—a holy people separate from other nations and identified as the people of God. This is an important thought, as we think about the New Testament and how the Church functions today. First Peter 2:9 says, *"But you are a chosen race, a royal priesthood, a holy nation, a people for his own possession, that you may proclaim the excellencies of him who called you out of darkness into his marvelous light."*

Here we see a progression from what God proclaimed to the people of Israel to the fulfillment of the New Testament Church being made up of all people being priests. We no longer need priests to be our mediators. Because of Jesus we all have direct access to communicate with God.

Now, reread Exodus 19:5–6 above. In order for the people of God to live up to the standard of a "priestly nation," they needed leadership, guidance, and help. This is why God established the Levitical priesthood from the line of Aaron to teach the people how to be a kingdom of priests. In other words, a nation set apart for God, intended to point others to Him.

This is the role of the modern-day Church. We are supposed to be set apart for God, to point everyone outside of the Church to God.

02   Think about your actions, words, attitudes, habits. What are some ways God asks you, or you have chosen, to be set apart in each of those areas?

But you are a chosen race,
a royal priesthood, a holy nation,
a people for his own possession,
that you may proclaim the excellencies
of him who called you out of darkness
into his marvelous light.

1 PETER 2:9

Thankfully, God equips us to live set apart. Reading and applying God's Word throughout the day, equips us to change our attitudes, actions, reactions, thoughts, words, and perspectives.

God also has set His Spirit in us. In the Old Testament the priests were anointed by oil as a public declaration of being set apart (Exodus 29). In the New Testament and even now, the people of God are anointed with the Holy Spirit who abides in them.

03   How does understanding this encourage and empower you?

Historically, there are three duties priests performed:

- Represent the people before God.
- Perform sacrifices.
- Provide counsel and structure.

These priests provided temporary access and intercession for the people of God, but they revealed a large hole that no one mortal, sinful, and imperfect individual could ever fill. The people of God still needed someone who could accomplish the role of a priest in completeness, which is exactly who Jesus is.

04   Read Hebrews 2:14–18. What does verse 17 refer to Jesus as?

While the Old Testament priests were God's faithful provision, Jesus embodies what they could never be: a High Priest without sin, yet completely able to empathize with the temptation of sin. In his book *Gentle and Lowly,* Dane Ortlund discusses not just what Jesus Christ has done but who Jesus is and His deepest heart for His people. Ortlund says it this way: "The various high priests through Israel's history were sinfully weak; Jesus the High Priest was sinlessly weak."[29]

05   Read Hebrews 4:14–16. Even though Jesus' sinlessness could make Him seem unapproachable for us, what do these verses instruct us to do anyway?

The blood of the sin offerings the priests made in the temple covered the sins from the community of people on the Day of Atonement, but as our High Priest, Jesus Himself was and is the sacrifice that made this possible and removes our sins through His own blood.

Instead of needing an external sacrifice, Jesus Himself was the sacrifice. He who knew no sin took on the sins of the world (2 Corinthians 5:21). The road to the cross He bore paved the way for a path of righteousness for us.

Remember the distinctives of what the Old Testament priests were to do? Represent the people before God, perform sacrifices, and provide counsel and structure. Let's look at how these things manifest in Jesus Himself:

1. **Jesus is the ultimate representative for humanity before God and intercedes for us.** (See Romans 8:34; Hebrews 7:25.)
2. **Jesus Himself was the Sacrificial Lamb, who made atonement in finality through the shedding of His own blood.** (See John 1:29; 1 John 2:2; Hebrews 1:3.)
3. **Jesus provides counsel and direction to us through the Holy Spirit, (John 14:26) who is the Spirit of Christ.** (See Philippians 1:19; Acts 16:7; Galatians 4:6.)

Let's close today by pausing to reflect on this truth: Because of Jesus, even when God feels absent, we still have full access to Him. This provision of direct access should forever remind us that we are significant. He wants us close because of His love of us, His intimate connection with us, and His important assignments for us.

Prophets

1 KINGS 18:16–1 KINGS 19:9 / LUKE 4:1–15

And Elijah came near to all the people and said, "How long will you go limping between two different opinions? If the LORD is God, follow him; but if Baal, then follow him."

1 KINGS 18:21

Have you ever prayed or cried out to God, asking Him to give you a picture of the future so you don't feel so shaken by today? I have. On one hand, I know God is in control and He can take everything and somehow work things together for good. But on the other hand, the good He is working out in the future isn't what I would consider good right now.

Eventual good doesn't ease the ache and heartbreak of today.

Eventual good can feel so far away you wonder if it will ever happen.

Eventual good doesn't make the panic of this moment less intense.

But what if all of our uncertainty of the future is because we haven't understood that Jesus is our prophet who assures us with certainty and guides us through hard circumstances and never abandons us?

I don't often think of Jesus as a prophet. But just as God gave Old Testament prophets special information to lead His people to good, we have Jesus leading us personally. He knows exactly how all of our tomorrows will play out. He's a guide who knows how to avoid treacherous terrain. He knows how we are feeling as humans with real fears, real heartbreak, real sorrow, real anxiety, and real effects of sin. He knows how to get from where we are today to the promised good God has in store.

That's why today's study is important for us. Remember, if we can see Jesus in unexpected ways in the Old Testament, we are more likely to believe He's working in the unseen places of our lives today.

So what was the role of the prophets in the Old Testament? And who are some of the prophets who point us to seeing Jesus as a prophet as well?

A prophet served as a mouthpiece and guide to the people of God. A prophet was God's gracious provision of assurance so His people didn't feel alone and wouldn't panic in the midst of unexpected circumstances. The prophets received a message from God and delivered this message to the people of God. This is known as *prophecy*.

01   What can you recall from Week 2 when we studied prophecy? Jot down a few thoughts.

Prophets spoke truth about present situations and identified punishment for evil or reward for righteous behavior. They were men *(navi')* and women *(navi'ah),* prophets and prophetesses, who were representatives of God.

And while we spent Week 2 looking at Old Testament prophecies that foretold the coming of Jesus, today we're going to study the Old Testament prophet Elijah and then see how Elijah's life compares and contrasts to the greater prophet, Jesus. We'll see how Jesus specifically and personally guides us, and through His guidance we can be filled with assurance and confidence.

Elijah was a prophet of God (1 Kings 18:36). Sometimes the Bible uses different words to describe the same thing. Another phrase we see used as a synonym for prophet is "man of God" *('ish ha'elōhim).*

"Man of God" identifies a person who is commissioned by God with a divine message to communicate to humanity (sometimes to the people of God, sometimes to foreign nations).

THIS PHRASE WAS USED TO DESCRIBE ELIJAH.

We can best understand the role of the prophet as that of a "mouthpiece" or a trumpet. Today, we may think of this like a microphone. While a microphone that is plugged into speakers can broadcast a message to a vast audience, the microphone is useless without the voice and breath of the person speaking into it.

This is what is happening with the prophets of the Old Testament, including Elijah. God is the voice and breath, the origin and source of the message, and His microphone is the prophets.

02   Read 1 Kings 18:16–1 Kings 19:9. What message did God send through Elijah? How did God show both His power and gentleness?

BEFORE WE GET TOO FAR, LET'S MAKE A CONNECTION BETWEEN THE PROPHET ELIJAH AND HOW HE IS A GLIMPSE OF JESUS.

GOD SENT JESUS, HIS OWN SON, TO GUIDE THE WORLD OUT OF THE DARKNESS AND DECEIT OF EVIL POWERS (FALSE GODS) AND BACK INTO THE FAMILY OF THE ONE TRUE GOD.

What the prophet Elijah does in this one incident of defeating evil, Jesus will accomplish in the ultimate defeat of evil for eternity.

Prophets were a great provision given to the people of God, but they also point to the greater provision of Jesus. While prophets like Elijah were seen as mouthpieces, Jesus as a prophet is not simply just the mouthpiece of God; He is God incarnate and therefore the very voice of God Himself.

God spoke through Elijah, and God showed His power by sending fire from Heaven. When Jesus speaks, God speaks.

When Jesus came from heaven, He brought the power of heaven to earth. We see an example of the greatness of Jesus as the better prophet in Matthew 4:1–11, in what's called a *"redemptive reversal." What a man like Elijah can only do in part and with human flaws, Jesus does in full with perfection. Take a look at the chart on the next page.

*A "redemptive reversal" can be defined as an image or description of a situation in the Bible that seems to be tragic but then, later in Scripture, is retold as a triumph. The tragic situation is reversed and redeemed and replaced with triumph.

Redemptive

ELIJAH (1 KINGS 19)	JESUS (MATTHEW 4:1–11; LUKE 4:1–12)
Elijah is led into the wilderness because of fear. 1 KINGS 19:3	Jesus is led into the wilderness by the Spirit. MATTHEW 4:1
Elijah looks for a way out of his plight. 1 KINGS 19:4	Jesus looks to God and is obedient in His plight. MATTHEW 4:1
Elijah is fed and taken care of by an *"angel of the LORD"* in the middle of his hunger and thirst. 1 KINGS 19:5–7	Jesus endures hunger in the wilderness. MATTHEW 4:2–4
The food Elijah eats sustains him throughout his 40-day journey because *"the journey is too great"* for him. 1 KINGS 19:7–8	Jesus endures 40 days of fasting and is tempted by the devil. The journey is not too great for Jesus, and after He is found faithful, the angels minister to Him. MATTHEW 4:11

And where did all of this provision take place? For both Elijah and Jesus, the provision occurred in the wilderness of the desert. In desert times, we often must face our inability to fix things on our own. We all must face the reality that we need the provision of God.

03　As you consider your own wilderness times, either of suffering or testing, how did you see God provide for you?

God gave the people of Israel a prophet in Elijah as a form of provision to guide them and fill them with assurance, and to remind them of the one true God of the heavens and the earth. But remember, Elijah was an imperfect prophet, not the perfect prophet. God sent the greatest provision in Jesus. He (and only He) is the ultimate prophet and the embodiment of confident assurance to us.

Provision in Kings

1 SAMUEL 8 / EPHESIANS 1

And the Lord said to Samuel, "Obey the voice of the people in all that they say to you, for they have not rejected you, but they have rejected me from being king over them."

1 SAMUEL 8:7

Hi friend. You and I have a lot in common. But I would imagine one of our most shared longings is to feel safe.

When we feel unsafe it can lead us to pursue anything we perceive will provide safety.

I have this struggle. When something happens and fear grips me, I can say things I wouldn't normally say. Or I can jump to worst-case scenarios and make decisions I wouldn't normally make.

Out of desperation, I can betray my best intentions. I want to trust God, but I want that threatening feeling to go away even more.

01   How do you personally relate to this? When has fear driven you to say or do things you wouldn't otherwise have said and done?

Sometimes the intentions we have are good, but the timing and motivation behind those intentions and desires can turn good things into reckless things. Which happened when Israel sought safety through an earthly king.

As we've learned, God was Israel's king. But the Israelites looked at the other countries. It seemed the others were better cared for by the presence of an earthly king than the presence of their God, whom they couldn't physically see. They feared the absence of an earthly king would leave them vulnerable. Their fear of their enemies was greater than their trust in God, so they went against God's warnings about an earthly king.

It can feel dysregulating when we feel unsafe. But **feelings should be indicators, not dictators.** Feelings should make us aware that something needs to be addressed, but feelings shouldn't dictate how we act and react.

Though the Israelites felt afraid, they were actually in the safest spot because they were led by God, who had supreme power, wisdom, and perfect intentions. God provided for all their needs and He was faithful to care for them. The biblical term for this idea is that Israel was ruled by a "theocracy."[30]

"Theocracy" comes from the Greek "θεός/theos," which means "God," and can be literally translated as "God rule."

THE JEWISH HISTORIAN JOSEPHUS FIRST USED THIS WORD TO DESCRIBE THE ISRAELITES AS BEING UNDER THE DIRECT RULE AND REIGN OF GOD.

God's provision is an overflow of who He is. Because God's character never changes, He will always provide for us. What the people of God didn't understand is that God was going to provide not just an earthly king but the ultimate eternal King: Jesus.

Let's use the framework of Israel asking for a king to teach us how to be more mindful of our motivations and why it's so important to trust in God's timing.

02   Read 1 Samuel 8:4–9. What's going on in the text here? Who are the people rejecting?

Feelings should be indicators, not dictators.

Samuel is the prophet of God at this time. But he's old and none of his sons are qualified to take over as prophet. So the people fear they'll be without their connection to God. In desperation, they come up with their own solution.

It's shocking when God acknowledges His people are rejecting Him. God is the perfect solution to their fear. Yet they reject the *perfect* solution because they prefer an *immediate* solution.

03 Read 1 Samuel 8:10–22. What does God warn about the dangers of an earthly king? What does this reveal about character of an earthly king?

The people of Israel failed to realize God was already the King they wanted and needed. He is the Righteous Judge and Divine Warrior leading them into battle and claiming victory—even eternal victory.

Plus, God had plans for the future King Jesus, but of course His Kingship would be established in God's timing. The people subverted that timing and took matters into their own hands by asking and pleading for a king to meet their *immediate* needs. And in turn, asking for a lesser version of what God had already provided and planned to provide through King Jesus.

04 Have you ever tried to change God's timing or sought to fulfill desires your own way?

Saul, the first king the people sought, appeared good on the outside but turned out to be a disaster. After Saul, we find a king who more closely matches the kind of leader God desires: David.

05   Read 2 Samuel 8:15. How is David's kingship described?

Let's take a look at these two words: *"justice"* and *"equity"* (also translated "righteousness" [v. 15]). When "justice" *(mishpat)* and "equity" *(tsadaqah)* are used together in the Old Testament, they are attributed to the character of God (Job 37:23; Psalm 33:5; Proverbs 8:20; Isaiah 5:16; Jeremiah 9:24; Micah 7:9).[31] God desired the kings of Israel to reflect His justice and righteousness.

Kings not only judged but went to battle on behalf of the people. Again, we find David as a king who matches this ideal to a degree. David's royal life is filled with heroic military exploits and accolades starting with the defeat of Goliath and the victory over tens of thousands of Philistines (1 Samuel 18:7–8; 1 Samuel 18:30; 1 Samuel 23:5; 2 Samuel 5:17–25). However, the narrator of 1 and 2 Samuel places a key phrase to coincide with David's victories.

06   Read 1 Samuel 18:14; 2 Samuel 5:10; and 2 Samuel 8:6,14. What is the key idea and what does this tell us about David's victories?

In each of these examples, we are reminded that God was with David. **What makes a king great is his nearness to the King of kings.** Human kingship had serious flaws but also created a deep awareness of the longing for something better. For someone better. And this ideal King could only be fully accomplished in Jesus, the one true King.

The New Testament shows that Jesus is the long-awaited King. However, Jesus would execute justice and equity in a different way: the shedding of His own blood to make the final atonement for sin. Jesus would enter into a cosmic battle with sin and death on the cross and would defeat death and remove the sting of sin through death itself. While David's body lay in a royal tomb, Jesus' body rose and walked out of the tomb.

As we wrap up, read Ephesians 1:18–21. As you consider the power Jesus displays as the King of kings, think about how this encourages you in the places of your heart that are struggling to feel safe.

TODAY, WE'VE SEEN HOW THE OLD TESTAMENT KINGS
LEFT THINGS SO UNFULFILLED. BUT IN JESUS, AS THE KING OF KINGS,

we have a King who rules sovereignly, and He's also there presently and personally.

When we read about the kings of the Old Testament, we can see a picture of Jesus being what the people of God were so desperate for all along.

Provision in Bread

EXODUS 16 / JOHN 6:31–35

———

For the bread of God is he who comes down from heaven and gives life to the world.

JOHN 6:33

It can be frustrating to race out the door, late for a meeting, and hear your stomach growl. The hurried pace of the morning and the emptiness of your stomach leaves you feeling not just hungry but *hangry*.

When physical needs arise, we can feel vulnerable and even desperate. While we may laugh at our tendency to become "hangry," these feelings from lack of physical supply are actually found in the Old Testament quite often.

For over 400 years in Egypt, God's people had been looking in many directions for their daily needs. They looked down at crops growing from the land. They looked at the available livestock for meat. And they looked to their Egyptian slave masters to be told when and how much they could eat. The Israelites were conditioned to look everywhere for their provision—except up.

Looking down and around was the opposite of looking up to God and trusting Him to be their provider.

The Egyptians had the Israelites working to construct all kinds of buildings, like temples and palaces. In order to keep watch over them, the Egyptian taskmasters stood on platforms and looked down on the Israelites as they worked. Platforms are always so deceptive because they make us feel bigger, better, and more powerful than we actually are. Just think about our day and age with the platforms of social media. With every like, comment, and share on Instagram it can feel like our platform is being built brick by brick (or like by like!). This is an important reminder for us not to look down at what we create but rather look up at what God provides.

When God delivered Israel from Egypt and into the wilderness, those provisions and slave masters were gone. The Israelites were free people. But as long as their routines were chained to old habits, thinking, and activities, they wouldn't experience real freedom.

So God used their most basic, daily need—food—to shift their hearts and minds. He took them to the desert, where they would not be able to look down, out, or to a person to get their needs met.

THEY WOULD HAVE TO LOOK UP.

01   How can you start practicing looking up to God more often for your daily provision?

02   Read Exodus 16:4. What does God say?

Israel's food would come from God alone. He would rain down enough bread each day to sustain them. They would have to develop a new daily habit, new thinking, and new activities in order to get their food. They would have to learn to look to God for everything in the wilderness.

03   Read Exodus 16:31. What type of bread God was going to provide for His people?

Every time the Israelites gathered the bread, they had an opportunity to look up to God and acknowledge Him as their provider. The daily ritual of gathering manna established new patterns of trusting God mentally and physically.

In Exodus 16:4, we are reminded that the One in heaven who provides rain, which sustains life in the long term, is also the One who sends bread, which sustains life daily! The manna coming from heaven was the fulfillment of God's promise to the Israelites. His presence and provision in their daily moments of need was also intended to train them to expect God to intervene and act in the same way in the future (Exodus 16:1–8).

The manna in the Old Testament was intended to stir anticipation for a manna that would be eternal in nature.

IN OTHER WORDS,

manna was a symbol for intermediate provision until the Bread from heaven came to bring true and eternal satisfaction.

In John 6:31–35, Jesus declares Himself as the Bread of Life. He makes a direct connection to Moses and the story of the manna in the wilderness. The Jews hearing Jesus must have known this story well. Manna saved their ancestors from impending death. Just as the ancient Israelites were taught to live a 24-hour cycle of reliance on Yahweh to provide the bread from heaven, Jesus reminds us there is something even better we can rely on 24 hours a day . . . Himself.

Jesus said it best:

"'For the bread of God is he who comes down from heaven and gives life to the world.' They said to him, 'Sir, give us this bread always.' Jesus said to them, 'I am the bread of life; whoever comes to me shall not hunger, and whoever believes in me shall never thirst'" (John 6:33–35).

Trusting in Jesus as the Bread of Life grows our dependence on Him for the daily bread we ask for.

When Jesus taught us to pray in Matthew 6, He said, *"Give us this day our daily bread..."* (v. 11). The Greek word for "daily" (ἐπιούσιον / *epiousion*) refers to the present but also the days to come.[32] So when we read Jesus' request for daily bread in the Lord's Prayer, we are invited to pray in hopeful anticipation for the future (the heavenly banquet) but also pray to be sustained in the present (manna).

Knowing Jesus as the Bread of Life creates an even deeper moment of meaning for us when we break bread during Communion.

In Luke 22:14–20 Jesus tells His disciples to remember, whenever they break bread in Communion, that the bread is a symbol of His body. Jesus connects and completes the image of manna as provision for the people of God in the wilderness, as His own body would be broken as a type of provision for all of humanity, for all those who repent of their sin and turn to Him. The people in the wilderness woke up hungry, but the person who remembers the body of Jesus, broken for her, will be reminded of the fullness of sacrifice, and as Jesus said, they will hunger and thirst no longer (John 6:35).

Remembering Jesus as the Bread of Life can comfort us in our own experiences of lack and longing.

God's provision may not be obvious or as expected. The Israelites certainly didn't expect food to come from heaven. And the timing of His provision may seem slow. During the 40 years the Israelites were in the desert, they didn't get the big, bountiful meals they wanted. That didn't come until they finally crossed over into the promised land. But God's provision was all around them each morning when the manna fell from heaven. The same is true for us. **Jesus is all around us, providing for us on a daily basis.**

God is providing. Jesus is faithfully with us in all of our needs. We are cared for. That has been the pattern of divine provision since the beginning of time. Take comfort in the fact that this will never change.

Provision in Water

EXODUS 17:1–6, JOHN 7:37–52

———

On the last day of the feast, the great day, Jesus stood up and cried out,
"If anyone thirsts, let him come to me and drink. Whoever believes in me,
as the Scripture has said, 'Out of his heart will flow rivers of living water.'"

JOHN 7:37–38

As we close this week on provision, think about the word "need." This word can contain an urgency and an angst. But the place of our greatest need is right where God will meet us. Our desperation and vulnerability create an opportunity for a divine appointment where God can reveal Himself to us and provide for our needs.

01　In what area of your life are you feeling vulnerable right now because of something you need?

Today, we are going to look at the crucial need every human has for water.

Perhaps the deepest vulnerability comes with unmet, daily physical needs like hunger and thirst. One of our most vital human needs is water. For the Israelites in the wilderness, when water seemed out of reach, they surely felt deprived and desperate.

Let's look at two examples of God providing water for the people of Israel.

Read Exodus 17:1–6 for the first example.

By this point in their exodus journey, the Israelites had been traveling for a few weeks. They'd seen God provide for their basic needs on countless occasions. Yet they turned from trusting in God to tormenting Moses with their quarrelsome and ungrateful words and behavior.

As the Israelites demanded water, God reminded both Moses and the people that the very staff that struck the Nile and turned it to blood, causing immense death, would now be used by God to provide water and sustain life. Moses was then told to strike the rock that would provide water for the people.

God's faithfulness in providing for His people's thirst held great potential for deeper trust between them. But the people of God wavered when God didn't immediately show them an obvious water supply. They suddenly wanted to go back to Egypt where water was easier to get, and they reframed the brutality of their past slavery as safe and secure (Exodus 16:3).

Now let's look at a second example of God providing water for His people which happened at the end of the wilderness journey.

Read Numbers 20:1–5.

Sound familiar? But God's instruction to Moses here was different than in Exodus when God told Moses to get water from the rock.

02   Read Numbers 20:6–9. What are God's directions to Moses?

03   Now read Numbers 20:10–13. What did Moses do instead?

Previously, in Exodus 17, God had instructed Moses to strike the rock. But here, God told Moses to speak to the rock. Moses' act of disobedience actually places him in the same state of rebellion as the quarrelsome Israelites. There is something important for us to notice here.

God wants us to follow His day-by-day direction rather than slipping into a pattern of just using past instructions from Him. God knows what we need today and wants to be in relationship with us so He can lead us situation to situation. God leads; we follow. That's the pattern we should commit to.

The Rod and the Rock

The rod and the rock were both present in these stories.

However, in the second instance God wanted Moses to speak to the rock. Instead, Moses struck the rock, and water flowed from it. In other words, in this second instance, provision for the people came through an act of aggression. However, the same object that is the victim of the aggression (the rock) is the source of the provision.

The Apostle Paul's words bring fulfillment to the image of the rock and the rod in a profound way in 1 Corinthians 10:1–4. Paul reflects on the story of the Israelites in the wilderness, identifying the rock of Exodus 17 and Numbers 20 as *Christ Himself.*

This is a mind-blowing connection that again helps us notice that the picture of the rock and the rod in these Old Testament stories was always intended to help us see a glimpse of Jesus.

In Matthew 27:29–30, Jesus is struck

(becoming a victim of aggression) as He is led away to be crucified. Jesus would be hung on the cross so that ultimately, through the pouring out of His very own blood, He would both physically and spiritually save all who place their trust in Him.

But seeing Jesus inside these stories doesn't just end there.

In John 7:37–52, we find Jesus not providing a physical source for water but declaring that He *Himself* is bringing the Living Water of God. He was declaring, just like He did over and over, that all of the Old Testament Scriptures point to *Him.*

We all have a physical thirst. But Jesus is speaking to an even deeper thirst we all have: the thirst in our soul that nothing else can ever satisfy. And the only thing He requires is that we recognize our deep need for Him and turn to Him.

04   Think about the spiritual thirst we just talked about. What does your soul really thirst for? Write out a prayer inviting Jesus into this need.

The stories of the Old Testament, especially these two stories, don't just reveal Jesus to us; they also remind us of God's faithfulness with our own deep longings and needs.

In the wilderness, God provided water for the Israelites. And even better, God provided, through Jesus, Living Water for anyone who would come and confess their thirst and need for eternal satisfaction. Even when we have unmet and unfulfilled longings, He has forever made a way.

And while we're in the wilderness of living with all the imperfections and devastations of a world full of sin, we will never go thirsty when we trust in Jesus. We all long for the perfection of heaven to invade earth, but while we wait, let's keep turning to Jesus, our only connection to perfection and satisfaction here in this world. The Living Water available to us today is yet an appetizer of what is to come.

*Father God, thank You so much for sending Your
Son, Jesus, as the ultimate Prophet, Priest, King,
Bread of Life, and Living Water. Seeing Him so
active and evident in Scripture brings me such
comfort in places of my heart that feel empty today.
Thank You for listening to my prayers for all the
things I desire, need, want, and ask for. I pray,
in the meantime, You sustain my faith by
reminding me of Your past faithfulness to always
keep Your promises. Thank You for the perfect
provision of Jesus that paved the way for a
relationship with You. In Jesus' Name, Amen.*

Protections

Since we're all friends now by Week 5 of the study, I just need to give you a little peek inside my brain.

I'm a happy and positive person mostly. But when I get afraid, I can think of worst-case scenarios quicker than just about anyone I know. It's not that I get doomsday-ish. I just want to brace myself for all possible outcomes of a situation.

Now, granted, in some cases being aware of possible dangers can help me take appropriate extra precautions. But letting my fears go unchecked can make me feel like I'm in a constant state of threat and emergency.

As I've watched this play out in my life, here's what I've learned: Collecting worst-case scenarios doesn't protect me. It only projects the possible pain of tomorrow into today and feeds more fear. And really, what it reveals to me is this: I have trouble trusting God as my ultimate protector.

If you struggle with this too, I think you're going to find these next few days very helpful.

Interestingly enough, using various images throughout the Old Testament, God is referred to as a protector. We see Him referred to as a fortress (Psalm 18:2), shield (2 Samuel 22:31), hiding place (Psalm 32:7), refuge (Psalm 91:2), shelter (Isaiah 25:4), and stronghold (Nahum 1:7).

These visual images are based on real places in Old Testament times that offered safe harbor in the midst of danger. A place to run when chaos threatened. They were also symbols of promised protection when things were peaceful. If there was ever any doubt about safety and security, these symbols and images served as a source of reassurance and were places of security and peace, to rest and recover.

The people of Israel needed physical places like these as protection from enemies, which is why so many cities had walls. Though we don't have walled cities with high towers for protection, we have symbols of protection all around us today. However, these security measures can only protect us to a certain extent. Ultimately, we need a God who offers His protection.

Thankfully our Divine Warrior is still fighting on our behalf. He hasn't abandoned His role as our protector. But His protection doesn't always look the same today as it did for the Israelites.

Sometimes we experience hardship and harm as a result of sin, both ours and others', and in these moments, we may wonder where God's protection is. We may look back at our lives and declare that God surely abandoned us in a time of greatest need. And if that's you, please know I get it. I sometimes have those same feelings as well.

Trying to understand and trust God as our protector, in the midst of a very fallen world, can be confusing and scary. In fact, it's one of the greatest areas of spiritual wrestling we will ever do. Even "giants" of our faith struggled with this paradox.

The psalms are filled with David's heartfelt cries of abandonment and fears around being so vulnerable to his enemies. In Psalm 13:1, David cries out, *"How long, O LORD? Will you forget me forever? How long will you hide your face from me?"*

But as we will see this week, God's protection comes in many forms— it's not always a physical removal of threat or a relief of emotional pain. Sometimes His protection is spiritual. Spiritual protection is what God is doing in the spiritual realm that we don't see. Remember Ephesians 6:12 (NIV): *"For our struggle is not against flesh and blood, but against the rulers, against the authorities, against the powers of this dark world and against the spiritual forces of evil in the heavenly realms."*

Throughout so many stories we've studied together, we've seen evidence eventually confirm that God was working things out in unseen ways. What first appeared to be God not rescuing someone in the short-run wound up ending differently. God was working behind the scenes for their protection in the long-run. God is never a do-nothing God. And the greatest assurance of that spiritual protection is found in Jesus Himself, who can see what is happening in both the physical and the spiritual realms at the same time and who is leading us, guiding us, and standing with us through it all.

As we study God's protection throughout Scripture, we'll start to see each of these moments as steps towards the ultimate protection we have in Christ Jesus.

It's fascinating to learn that some people in the Old Testament serve as shadows and types of the greater Protector to come: Jesus. These people were hand-picked by God, which was demonstrated in unusual, unexplainable, unlikely, and unique ways, but always ended in unchanging protection for the Israelites.

If you are a highlighting kind of person, mark these five words: **unusual, unexplainable, unlikely, unique, and unchanging.** Those words will be important in the new perspectives we will gain this week around God's protection and how we can more clearly see Jesus in the midst of it all.

This week as we study, we will find that God works to protect those He loves. Who does God love? The people He created in His likeness and image . . . including you and me. Each day we will gain greater revelations of God's goodness through His protection and find that Jesus was at the center of each of these moments, in either visible or hidden ways. Regardless, He was there. And if He was there in those moments, we can be assured that Jesus is with us in the moments when we need His protection.

Protection of Joseph

As for you, you meant evil against me, but God meant it for good,
to bring it about that many people should be kept alive, as they are today.

GENESIS 50:20

I like God's protection to be completely obvious and immediate. This can cause me to miss His care and wrongly think He's not there for me. That's why looking at the story of Joseph again is very helpful.

We've already looked at the big picture of Joseph's life, but today, we'll take a more focused look at the shift he made from being wounded to being a protector. This is another example of how the story of Joseph shows us Jesus. Jesus also experienced relational wounding, abandonment, betrayal, and rejection by the very ones He eventually saved.

Let's not miss the fact that Joseph is a person, not just a character in a story. Some of the very same reactions we have to our pain must have been there for Joseph as well. The fear, anxiety, uncertainties, worrying, and trying to stay hopeful when every circumstance around him just seemed to point to hopelessness. I'm especially curious about how he shifted his perspective from being consumed with the unfairness of it all to trusting God with the unfolding of it all.

First, let's look at a place in Scripture where Joseph speaks about the unfairness and angst of what's happened to him while still in prison. Read Genesis 40:15.

01   How do you relate to this statement from Joseph?

Next read Genesis 41:1 and then verse 14. This happens two years after Joseph spoke the statement about not deserving to be in this prison. Two long years where I'm sure Joseph once again felt abandoned and so incredibly hopeless. And then, in a moment, everything turns around: *". . . Pharaoh sent for Joseph, and he was quickly brought from the dungeon"* (Genesis 41:14a NIV). In this crucial conversation Joseph has with Pharaoh, something incredible happens.

When Pharaoh asks Joseph if he can interpret his dream, Joseph says no. This was Joseph's big moment to shine in front of the one who had the power to change his situation! Instead, Joseph puts his faith in God on display: *"'I cannot do it,' Joseph replied to Pharaoh, 'but God will give Pharaoh the answer he desires'"* (Genesis 41:16 NIV). After interpreting Pharaoh's dreams, Joseph impresses him so much with his wisdom and discernment that Joseph is promoted to become the second most powerful man in Egypt.

God had absolutely been working through Joseph's hardships to develop in him everything he would need to step into a calling that would save many lives. Joseph gained more wisdom and discernment than Pharaoh had seen in anyone else.

02   As you think about some of your hardships right now, what good qualities might God be developing in you?

God wasn't just developing Joseph's character. He would eventually use what Joseph went through to be a protection for the people of Egypt and the Israelites as well.

Now, read Genesis 45:1–8. This is the moment when Joseph no longer hides his identity from his brothers. Pay close attention to the perspective shift Joseph reveals in verses 5 and 8. Not only is he starting to see his experience as God's unlikely way of protecting him, but he's also seeing some greater purpose as well.

03   What was the greater purpose of Joseph's pain? How does this encourage you to also look for some purpose in your pain?

Joseph was able to see beyond the pain to God's purpose, as we see when he speaks these words to his brothers: *"As for you, you meant evil against me, but God meant it for good, to bring it about that many people should be kept alive, as they are today"* (Genesis 50:20).

The story of Joseph teaches us that God's protection sometimes comes in ways we might misunderstand. Instead of being tempted to wrongly think God is being cruel or uncaring, maybe we can believe He's developing our character to prepare us for a much bigger protection than we can fathom.

Now, before we throw a celebration of all the good we can learn from Joseph, I think it's valuable to also learn from some not-so-good choices he made.

Everything is going as planned. Joseph is thriving and God's people are thriving. Joseph has every reason to be generous with the nation that has enabled all this thriving. We would expect, maybe even hope, that Joseph would show the Egyptians the same empathy, love, and compassion he shows to the Israelites. But Joseph's treatment of the Egyptians in the midst of a famine shows us a different side.

04   Read Genesis 47:13–20. Summarize what Joseph chooses to do. What might his motivations
        have been?

It wasn't that Joseph was blatantly sinning, but he acted in ways that weren't in line with the compassion he could have extended toward others. In contract, Jesus, the greater Joseph, offers protection to all people who turn to Him without carrying any bias or prejudice or personal agenda.

Let's look at Hebrews 5:2, and verses 7–9. The author of Hebrews tells us that Jesus in His humanity learned obedience through His suffering. Remember, that while Jesus was sinless, He knew the pain of being sinned against. Ultimately, as these verses point out, the weakness, suffering, and obedience of Jesus leads Him to deal gently with us.

The Greek word for "learned" (ἔμαθεν, *emathen*) in Hebrews 5:8 suggests a process.[33] Jesus didn't simply arrive without enduring affliction. He willingly submitted Himself to the process that would lead to suffering. But the suffering and weakness of Jesus resulted in a deep awareness and empathy for the hardship of those around Him.

This is another area where Jesus is the greater Joseph. Jesus lived a life of perfection and endured pain and suffering not for just one people group or ethnicity but for all people groups and ethnicities. Jesus' death, burial, resurrection, and ascension is an act of redemptive reversal. Unlike Joseph, who enslaved those who were not his own, Jesus redeems, restores, and reclaims all people who turn from their sin and turn towards Him as the Messiah.

This is exactly what Paul says in Galatians 4:3–7: *"In the same way we also, when we were children, were enslaved to the elementary principles of the world. But when the fullness of time had come, God sent forth his Son, born of woman, born under the law, to redeem those who were under the law, so that we might receive adoption as sons. And because you are sons, God has sent the Spirit of his Son into our hearts, crying, 'Abba! Father!' So you are no longer a slave, but a son, and if a son, then an heir through God."*

05   Has Jesus ever redeemed/restored/released you from any form of "captivity"? Things that hold us captive can be thought processes, fears, addictions, etc. How have you experienced God's protection in this way?

Joseph looked out for his own family, but Jesus made a way for all to be invited and included into the family of God. Not only have we been set free from the bondage of sin, but we were also granted the status of sons of God. Jesus does for you and I what Joseph could never do. Jesus elevates us as royal children of the King of heaven and earth. The great promise of this adoption by God, as Paul says in these verses, is that the Spirit of Jesus was sent to us as a sign and symbol of our future inheritance.

Protection in the Red Sea

EXODUS 14 / MARK 4:35–41

And he awoke and rebuked the wind and said to the sea, "Peace! Be still!" And the wind ceased, and there was a great calm. He said to them, "Why are you so afraid? Have you still no faith?"

MARK 4:39–40

Trust is delicate. It's hard to earn and easy to lose. Trusting someone else takes time. Especially when it comes to our own protection. We were designed with a high level of awareness around our need for self-protection, and at the slightest threat, we fight, fly, or freeze.

If someone breaks our trust, we naturally become guarded. When someone proves they are trustworthy, our confidence in them grows and we feel safe enough to let our guard down. Why? Because there is a consistent pattern of faithfulness demonstrated.

This is the kind of trust Moses developed with God. He could trace God's past faithful protection over and over. Moses had seen God help him do what seemed impossible: leading the Israelites out of captivity in Egypt. Just when there seemed to be no way Pharaoh would ever heed Moses' demand to let the people go, God demonstrated His *unexplainable* protection by using His power over nature to get Pharaoh's attention. God unleashed 10 plagues over Egypt, which eventually convinced Pharaoh to let the Israelites go.

Then God demonstrated His unexplainable protection again when He led the people in a less direct path to the promised land: *"But God led the people around by the way of the wilderness toward the Red Sea"* (Exodus 13:18a).

Exodus 14:4 reveals God's plan to yet again show His people His ability to protect them: *"'And I will harden Pharaoh's heart, and he will pursue them, and I will get glory over Pharaoh and all his host, and the Egyptians shall know that I am the LORD.' And they did so."*

Just as God planned, with the Egyptians marching after them, the Israelites found themselves facing an angry sea in front of them and an angry enemy behind them. The only way for them to be saved would be for God to do something that could never have even been dreamed up with the human mind . . . Again it was God's *unexplainable* protection.

Israel's Path and God' Protection

**GOD UNLEASHES
10 PLAGUES OVER EGYPT**

EXODUS 5:1–11

**PHAROAH LETS
ISRAELITES GO**

EXODUS 12:31–42

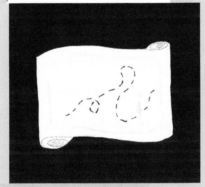

**ISRAELITES ON
WANDERING PATH**

EXODUS 13:17–22

**PHAROAH / EGYPTIANS
COMING AFTER ISRAELITES**

EXODUS 14:5

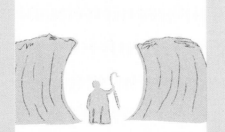

**PARTING OF
THE RED SEA**

EXODUS 14:19–31

Read Exodus 14:10–12.

01   What does the people's response to Moses show about their mental and emotional state?

Notice a common thread in the reaction of the Israelites as we've been studying together? Let's also not forget there was more going on. The Israelites were not left alone or unprotected.

Read Exodus 14:13–14.

02   We don't have a record of the people's response after hearing Moses' direction. What would your response have been?

The initial response after crying out to God to fight on their behalf was silence. The Israelites surely thought Moses' advice made no sense. However, Moses was leading the people to use silence as a spiritual discipline. Moses told the people to sit silent and watch God protect them and fight on their behalf. If we were the Israelites, we would have probably demanded an explanation for what seemed like such an odd response to such a serious threat.

As we consider our own use of silence in the midst of threats, there can be many benefits. One purpose of silence may be to focus on the simplicity of God's power over all things. Another benefit might be to quiet distractions and interruptions that tempt us to explain away God's protection in our lives.

MAYBE SILENCE AND SOLITUDE ARE WAYS FOR US TO PROCESS AND
FIND PEACE WITH THINGS THAT SEEM SO UNEXPLAINABLE IN OUR LIVES.

Maybe silence and solitude are ways for us to **process and find peace** with things that seem so unexplainable in our lives.

What would happen if we practiced the spiritual discipline of silence today by spending focused time meditating on the protection and provision of God in our lives? What if we intentionally remembered to trace God's faithfulness in the past until it helped us feel more safe and secure in the faithful and secure hands of God? The Israelites were aware of this truth through tangible and visible examples but, in that moment, needed to pause and remember.

Read Exodus 14:19–20.

03   Who was also with the Israelites? Describe what was happening.

The end of the story is the protection of Israel through God's powerful authority over nature itself. God splits the Red Sea in half and creates a passageway of safety for His people to find rescue and deliverance.

As one Old Testament scholar has said, "Israel's escape route became a classroom for them, a period of testing in time and space that shaped the people Yahweh was making."[34]

Read Exodus 14:15–18.

04   Scripture demonstrates that sometimes God allows trials in order to reveal His power. Why would God work this way?

The experience at the Red Sea was a formative experience, helping the people of God better understand and live out trust in their Creator.

When we think about Jesus there are so many connections back to the Red Sea. The Israelites faced the Red Sea which was a sign/symbol of death, chaos, and disorder. Jesus faced the cross, a sign/symbol of death. The Israelites had to go through the Red Sea. Jesus had to go through the cross. On the other side of the Red Sea was the promised land for the Israelites. Jesus victory over sin and death brings the promise of the new heavens and new earth to those of us that put our trust and faith in Christ.

The more we remember what Jesus has done for us and what it means for us, the more we will be assured of His absolute devotion to protecting us.

Every moment we are with God, we are with His protection whether we realize it or not. And part of that protection, if we will trust Him and stay with Him, is how He will form us and shape us through what we experience.

05   Read 1 Corinthians 15:49. What is the goal of all of this shaping and forming?

The more we are shaped and formed to be like Jesus, the more we will be confident in God's protection. But even more than being confident, with Jesus we can have unexplainable peace in the process. Philippians 4:7 reminds us of this truth: *"And the peace of God, which surpasses all understanding, will guard your hearts and your minds in Christ Jesus."*

As we conclude today, let's turn to one more story involving another sea. In this New Testament story, found in Mark 4, Jesus is asleep on a boat in the middle of a storm on the Sea of Galilee. This is the type of storm that would put true fear in even the most seasoned sailors. In a moment of desperation, the disciples cry out to Jesus to provide protection for them. Jesus simply wakes up, rebukes the wind, and tells the sea to be still.

Simply the presence of Jesus and the voice of Jesus in the midst of the storm establishes peace. Where Jesus is present, peace is possible.

This doesn't mean there won't be storms, trials, tribulations, and hardships. Certainly the children of Israel and Moses experienced these. The disciples in the New Testament experienced these. And we will, too. But we are never left alone He is with us. With Jesus, even when our circumstances don't feel peaceful, we can choose to do things His way and, in doing so, have peace that passes all understanding.

And in the end, if we will just remember to reflect on the many ways we've seen God move in our past and the peace available to us in the present, we can know we are being protected.

Protection in Jonah

JONAH 1 / MATTHEW 8:23-27

———

And the men marveled, saying, "What sort of man is this, that even winds and sea obey him?"
MATTHEW 8:27

Have you ever had a very normal day suddenly take a hard turn?

If anyone could relate to this reality, it was Jonah. I doubt you've ever thought that being swallowed by a whale would be protection. But this is exactly what happened with Jonah.

In Jonah's story, we will learn that the safest place to be is always within the will of God, no matter how unsafe it might look. And sometimes God protects us from ourselves in surprising ways. For Jonah, God provided some protection through a U-turn that landed him in the belly of a fish.

The story of Jonah has another very important connection, and that's between Jonah and Jesus. First, let's review Jonah's story.

Jonah was a prophet from Gath Hepher in Galilee (in Samaria) and prophesied in the northern kingdom of Israel. He's one of the 12 minor prophets and one of only a handful that Jesus personally referenced (Matthew 12:41). But what stands out most about Jonah is that he's also the only prophet who tried to run from God.

The book of Jonah opens with God's command to go to Nineveh and *"call out against it, for their evil has come up before me"* (Jonah 1:2). Nineveh was an important city and the Ninevites were enemies of the Israelites. The majority of biblical references to Nineveh portray the city as evil (Jonah 1:2) and destined to experience doom (Nahum 2:8; Nahum 3:7; Zephaniah 2:13).

With Nineveh's reputation for evil, it's no wonder Jonah was reluctant to declare God's message there. So, instead of going to Nineveh, Jonah boarded a boat in Joppa headed west to Tarshish. This was 2,500 miles in the opposite direction, by way of a sea.

Jonah didn't get very far in his journey before a storm arose.

Read Jonah 1:1–5.

01 Throughout all this chaos, confusion, and danger, where is Jonah? What does this tell us about his state of mind?

Read Jonah 1:6.

This must have been quite a storm if seasoned sailors were afraid. Finally, the only solution is to throw Jonah into the sea. God saves Jonah, but that protection comes in the form of a great fish or "whale," as it is translated in some versions of the Bible.

Jonah 1:17a says that *"the Lord appointed a great fish to swallow up Jonah."* This is not by chance. God's action always has purpose, and his motivation here is protection. God still has work for Jonah to do, and He uses the belly of the whale to teach and lead Jonah.

02 Can you recall a time where God protected you by redirecting your path and placing you in a holding pattern? What did you learn during that time?

We also shouldn't miss the language of the *"belly"* of the whale (Jonah 1:17b). The Hebrew word used here is *me'eh*. The same word is used in Genesis 15:4 and Ruth 1:11 to describe the womb of a woman.

This choice of language might be to give us a picture of Jonah entering a time of learning, growing, and developing so that a new person might emerge. In other words, the imagery may be intended to show us that Jonah went through a type of rebirth or "baptism."

Baptism symbolically represents the process of spiritual death redeemed into spiritual life. In a similar way, Jonah enters the water as a doubt-filled and rebellious person and is intended to come out of the water a new person filled with faith and living a life of obedience. As we continue to read, we find this isn't exactly what happens with Jonah.

After Jonah's time in the fish, God gives him a second chance to obey.

Read Jonah 3:1–3.

> 03   What is Jonah's response to the Lord's word this time?

The people of Nineveh respond to Jonah's warning that their city will be overthrown. They call a fast and repent, *"from the greatest of them to the least of them"* (Jonah 3:5b). The response is so complete that the king of Nineveh joins his people and calls for a city-wide turning from evil ways. God relents and the Ninevites are saved.

Read Jonah 4:1–3.

Yet, rather than being relieved that God protected him from the evil Ninevites, Jonah has a different response.

> 04   Why might Jonah have reacted this way?

It's very possible Jonah was looking forward to watching God pour down His wrath on his enemies. As obedient as Jonah eventually was, his actions and words revealed his true heart and motivations. Here is where we see Jesus, the better Jonah.

Jesus, just like Jonah, found Himself asleep on a boat in the middle of the sea during a storm (Matthew 8:23–27). But unlike Jonah, who was thrown out of the boat in order for the storm to cease, Jesus, the greater Jonah, commanded the storm to cease.

Jesus, just like Jonah, found Himself in the darkness of a deep abyss (the grave) for three days. But unlike Jonah, who was sent into the belly of the whale forcefully, Jesus willingly humbled Himself, even to the point of death, and stayed in a tomb for three days. There was no need for an image of death (the sea) because Jesus experienced the very realness of death.

Jesus, just like Jonah, continued His ministry on earth for a period of 40 days (Acts 1:3) after His three days in the tomb. Jesus willingly and joyfully provided forgiveness, salvation, and reconciliation for all people from all nations. And He commanded the disciples to go out to the ends of the earth, making disciples from among the nations (Matthew 28:18–20). But Jonah begrudgingly went to Nineveh and was disappointed when God relented and forgave them.

Jesus, just like Jonah, was intimately connected to the most unexpected image that would lead to the protection and reconciliation of many. For Jonah, that unexpected image was a fish. For Jesus, that unimaginable image was the cross.

As Andrew Knowles points out: "Jonah gives us one of the Bible's great images of God's power to save. Just as Joseph was rescued from prison to become prime minister, and Daniel was kept safe among lions, Jonah is preserved in the belly of a great fish. These episodes prepare us for their greatest sequel— the resurrection of Jesus from the tomb. Jesus went down into the depths of death and experienced utter loss of God—but was raised as the ultimate proof of salvation."[35]

Today, it is the unlikely symbol of the cross that reminds us of God's love and protection for us. For it was on the cross that Jesus, the Son of God, paid the price for our sins. As we close today, write out a prayer on the following pages thanking Jesus for protecting us in this way.

Jesus willingly and joyfully
provided forgiveness,
salvation, and reconciliation
for all people from
all nations.

DR. JOEL MUDDAMALLE

My Prayer

Protection of the Torah

LEVITICUS 26 / HEBREWS 8:1–5

———

And beginning with Moses and all the Prophets, he interpreted to them
in all the Scriptures the things concerning himself.

LUKE 24:27

When I was growing up, my mom always gave me her "words of warning." Every time she started to share her wisdom, my natural impulse was to roll my eyes, let my mind drift to some random thought and just endure the "lecture" so I could get myself out of the situation and on with the more important things in my life.

Today, I realize those "words of warning" weren't random thoughts. My mom addressed things she saw in my life that concerned her. She knew if I didn't address the issues at hand, I might go down a dark road that would be very difficult to recover from.

In the Old Testament, God gave us words of warning as well. The first five books of the Bible are called the "Pentateuch," or the "Torah," which can be translated as "the books of the Law." Moses is traditionally believed to be the author of these books and they are key in our understanding of how God has worked in unique ways throughout history in the lives of His people to provide protection. We can also see Jesus in the middle of this protection as well.

"Torah," the first five books that make up a larger narrative story that includes principles from the Law.

"The Law" the rules, regulations, and commandments that were given to Israel and generally refer to (but aren't limited to) the commandments given in the wilderness of Sinai (Exodus 19–20).

You may be wondering: Why are we even discussing the Torah, and why should we care about the Law? Aren't both of these things obsolete in light of the New Testament? Well, no.

If we ignore or dismiss the Torah and the Law, we will actually miss the fulfillment and completion of both that comes in Jesus, the Messiah. The Torah's purpose wasn't just to record the Law, it was to get us through the Law and its brokenness, and finally to the greater promise and fulfillment in the Messiah in the last days.[36]

This is why the Torah and the Law are important to us. When we journey through the Torah, we find it actually leads us to Jesus the Messiah. By serving as a provisional (limited-time) protector of the people of God, the Torah enables us to see Jesus as the embodiment of all that the Torah points to, the "Word" that has become flesh in Christ (John 1). Jesus makes a startling statement in Matthew 5:17 when He says He didn't come to abolish the law but to fulfill it! This is yet another way we see Jesus in the Old Testament. Jesus fulfills the Torah and all the requirements of the Law.

Today, we'll take a look at three unique ways the Torah serves as a **guardian,** as a **shadow** and as a conduit of **wisdom.** This will help us see God's protection through the Torah.

THE TORAH AS GUARDIAN

Read Galatians 3:24.

Paul says something remarkable: The Law was meant to be our guardian. What does a guardian do but protect, care for, and instruct? This means that the Torah should be viewed as a gift of guardianship given to the people of God in order to tutor and train them in the ways to live and love. However, there was a time and season for the Torah to function, and that season as a guardian and tutor came to completion at the arrival of the Messiah, Jesus.

01   What are some ways the Law of God serves as a guardian in your life? How has God protected you through His Truth?

Read Hebrews 8:1–5.

Part of the Torah and Law includes rules and regulations for the priests and the temple of God. But as the author of Hebrews says, these things (the Torah, Law, priests, and temple) were all but a *"copy"* or a *"shadow"* (Hebrews 8:5) intended to point us to the substance behind the shadows. In earlier weeks we talked about how shadows prove that there is a sun. In this instance, again, we can see that the substance behind the shadow (Torah/Law) is none other than Jesus. Without Jesus, the priests, the temple, and all the laws would be unfulfilled or empty. But when we see Jesus as the substance, we can see and experience the full meaning and value of all of these things.

02   In addition to God's holy Word, the Bible, what things on earth serve as a shadow of heavenly things?

Read Hebrews 8:6–7.

03   What might the author of Hebrews mean when he says Christ's covenant is *"enacted on better promises"* (v. 6)?

We don't need to guess at what substance is behind the shadows of the Torah because the author of Hebrews says it plainly: Christ is better! And with Christ comes the fullness of the new covenant that illuminates the shadows of the old covenant (as seen in the Torah/Law), bringing completion and fulfillment.

THE TORAH AS WISDOM

Read 1 Corinthians 9:8–10.

This may seem like an odd text, but Paul is pointing out that the Law was not written for oxen but for us! We are to apply the Law and Torah through the lens of wisdom, which is God-given. In other words, "The Law is an expression of God's great wisdom."[37]

But we may ask: How is this wisdom to be applied and lived out? Well, once again the Torah and Law become very important.

Read Matthew 22:36–40.

04   Summarize Matthew 22:36–40 in your own words.

What is the heart of the Law? To love God and love others.

As Christians, our love for others should be framed first and foremost by our love for God. And it's through relationships with others where we apply the wisdom of the Bible and demonstrate real love. As we live a life of biblical love, we are fulfilling the heart of the Law.

As we wrap up today's study, let's read one more verse about how Jesus points to the Torah:

Read Luke 24:27.

Jesus was reading the writings of Moses (the Torah) and showed how all these passages were in fact pointing to Himself. In other words, Jesus was the teacher and tutor who fulfilled all the requirements of the Torah. In doing so, Jesus invites us to look to Him as we live a life reflective of the gospel, marked by love, and filled with the wisdom of Jesus.

Protection by the Divine Warrior

ISAIAH 59:1–20 / EPHESIANS 6:10–17

Finally, be strong in the LORD and in the strength of his might. Put on the whole armor of God,
that you may be able to stand against the schemes of the devil.

EPHESIANS 6:10–11

Throughout the ages, God's people have cried out for God to intervene in unfair situations. Because we are created in the image of God, there is something deep within us that longs for the scales of justice to weigh equal. We want the innocent to be redeemed and those who are guilty to pay amends.

If we've been hurt by injustice, we feel the pain intensely. Sometimes it seems like the guilty go unpunished while we pay the price. This can make us feel like God just doesn't care.

But in our final day of study this week, we will learn that God does not overlook these gross violations. In earlier weeks we discussed issues like injustice and the desire of God to see righteousness and mercy enacted by His people. Today, we will see that God is intently watching the plight of humanity, and He is not a complacent bystander. When it comes to issues of justice, God reveals Himself as our Divine Warrior.

In the book of Isaiah, we see a pattern of injustice. But we also see God's heartache and concern over it. These issues come to a head in Isaiah 58–59, when after observing all the injustice (the lack of truth and rampant mockery of righteousness), the Divine Warrior God, Yahweh, would have no more.

Read Isaiah 59:1–16.

01   In this passage, what issues incite God's anger regarding injustice?

This section of Scripture is often referred to as the "Divine Warrior Hymn."[38] Old Testament scholar John Goldingay reminds us that it is intended to bring to mind the victorious actions of God at creation (remember the image of the sea and chaos and how God brings order) and the deliverance at the Red Sea, and it also anticipates a future deliverance and victory that will come. It's this last anticipation that we want to hold on to and tuck away.

The specific phrase *"his own arm,"* found in verse 16, is loaded with meaning. The "arm" is a common metaphor used throughout the Old Testament to communicate the power of God in human history. We see this especially in Exodus and Deuteronomy (Exodus 6:6; 15:16; Deuteronomy 4:34; 5:15; 7:19; 9:29; 11:2; 26:8; Psalm 77:15).[39]

The phrase "his own arm" would have reminded the Israelites that what was about to happen is evidence of an unchanging and consistent God. It is a continuation of the divine and protective work of God.

When God sees the injustice mentioned in Isaiah 59:15, He prepares to address it in a specific way.

Read Isaiah 59:17.

> 02   What does Yahweh put on? Do you see any significance in the order of what God uses to prepare Himself for action?

Of all the things Yahweh puts on, let's focus on the cloak *(me'il)*. The Hebrew word translated into "cloak" was a type of clothing used for prophets (1 Samuel 15:27; Ezra 9:3, 5), priests (Exodus 28:4; Leviticus 8:7), and kings or royalty (1 Samuel 18:4; 24:5, 11; Ezekiel 26:16).

The imagery of a cloak causes us to reflect on the Messiah who would be our great Prophet, Priest, and King. The unchanging nature of God is shown in the unchanging consistency of Jesus. As we've seen throughout this study, we have seen reflections of Jesus through prophets, priests, and kings.

Jesus is here in every way we need Him. Just like the prophets, He speaks to us. Just like the priests, He prays and intercedes for us. Just like the kings, He leads and cares for us. But remember, the humans who filled these roles could only do in part what Jesus did in perfection. Therefore, His protection over us in all these ways is also perfectly consistent and unchanging as well. So, when our feelings beg us to believe differently, we can mark this study as the place to return to Truth.

Read Isaiah 59:18–20.

03   What will happen when God steps in to enact justice? What does verse 19 tell us about God's motive for repaying those who have turned from His ways?

The fact that the Divine Warrior is dealing with the root issue of sin should cause us to step back and consider who this Divine Warrior figure may be. The clues seem to indicate that the Divine Warrior is in fact the pre-existent and unchanging Warrior-King of heaven and earth, King Jesus. It is finally King Jesus who on the cross vanquishes sin and death. It is King Jesus in Revelation who ushers in the new heavens and new earth, where injustice will have no place and the Kingdom will be set up in righteousness and justice. It very well may be that the Divine Warrior is none other than the God-man, King Jesus.

But something else is also taking place. Today, you and I are being invited into the protection of the Divine Warrior. In Ephesians 6, Paul outlines the armor of God and its protection for us.[40]

Read Ephesians 6:13–17.

04   List the ways the armor of God protects us.

Notice anything similar? Paul is not referencing some arbitrary armor; rather it seems that he has in mind the very armor of the Divine Warrior, King Jesus. Within this story we find a redemptive reversal. Remember, a redemptive reversal is when God steps in and turns something that was once harmful or hurtful into something good and helpful.

Here in Ephesians 6, you and I, the children of God, are told to wear the armor of the King. However, before we are ever told to wear the armor we are told that we are protected by the guardian Holy Spirit (Ephesians 1:13–14).

Read Ephesians 6:10–12.

The phrases *"be strong in the LORD"* and *"in the strength of His might"* (v. 10) recall earlier references to the Spirit who raised Christ from the dead and seated Him at the right hand of the Father (Ephesians 1:19–20). This is the same Spirit that strengthens, equips, empowers and enables us to *"put on"* (Ephesians 6:11), *"take up"* (Ephesians 6:13), and *"take"* (Ephesians 6:17) the armor of the King.

05   As we close today, how does the unchanging protection of the Divine Warrior specially help you process something you're facing today?

AS WE WRAP UP, TODAY LET'S MAKE
AN INTENTIONAL DECISION TO
KEEP OUR MINDS FIXED ON THE
UNCHANGING NATURE OF JESUS.
AS WE THINK UPON JESUS AND THE
WAY HE ACTS THROUGH LOVE TO
BRING JUSTICE AND RIGHTEOUSNESS,
KINDNESS, AND COMPASSION,
LET'S MAKE THE DECISION TO JOIN
HIM IN HIS UNCHANGING WAYS.
NOW, LET'S PRAY TOGETHER:

Lord, thank You that You sent Jesus, who deeply understands how hard it can be to process fear inside these frail, hurting, human hearts of ours. Thank You for the hope that Jesus has overcome the world. Now help me overcome what I'm facing today. Thank You for the grace that I don't have to do it perfectly. I just have to make progress. I love You, Lord. In Jesus' Name, Amen.

Presence

When was the last time you played hide-and-go-seek?

Whether it was many years ago as a child yourself or fairly recently as a parent or babysitter, hide-and-seek is a timeless game filled with surprise.

It's funny watching small children play when they think if their eyes are covered and they can't see the "seeker," then the "seeker" must not be there. If they can't hear the "seeker" approaching the crowded space they're hiding in, then the "seeker" must not be there.

As we've written this study, we've thought about this image so many times.

Just because we can't always see Jesus doesn't mean He isn't there.
Just because we aren't hearing Him doesn't mean He's being silent.

Maybe you needed to read those last two sentences as much as we did. We wrote them not because it's easy for us to believe but because it's quite the opposite sometimes.

When the circumstances we face feel crushing, scary, confusing, or truly just impossible to figure out, how can we know that Jesus really is with us?

Since you're in Week 6 now, we hope you can respond to the question with the confident assurance of this answer: Because He always has been. And it's more than a promise for the future. It's a reality right now. Jesus is actively with us.

A significant takeaway from this whole study for us has been the reality that if we can see Jesus' presence in the Old Testament, beyond a prophecy of the Messiah's coming, then we can have deeper conviction He is present in our lives right now, too.

It's surprising how explicit the New Testament authors are about Jesus' presence in the Old Testament:[41]

- The "I Am" in whom Abraham rejoiced was Jesus (John 8:56–58).
- The Lord who motivated Moses was Christ (Hebrews 11:26).
- The Redeemer who brought God's people out of Egypt was Jesus (Jude 5).
- The Rock in the wilderness was Christ (1 Corinthians 10:4).
- The King of Isaiah's temple vision was the Son (John 12:40–41).

Jesus is not merely patterned, pointed to, and promised in the Old Testament, He is present.

And the same is true in our life right now. He is present. Jesus is never hiding from us. He's waiting to be seen by us.

Sometimes in moments when we're overwhelmed with life, we can find ourselves saying, "Today would be a really good day for Jesus to come back." But in reality, He's already here, right now. Yes, He will return as the victorious King in physical form one day. But for today, He's here.

Rest in that and be so very assured of that truth as you dive into what God has for you in this final week.

The Tabernacle and the Temple

EXODUS 25:1–9 / EPHESIANS 2:19–22

———

And the Word became flesh and dwelt among us, and we have seen his glory,
glory as of the only Son from the Father, full of grace and truth.

JOHN 1:14

Have you ever stood on the sidelines of a sporting event?

Whether you're at a Little League game or in the stands at a collegiate or professional match, there is nothing like being in the environment of an exciting, competitive event.

Simply put, I'm in the season of life where all of my children want to try every single sport: winter, spring, summer and fall. Which basically tells you I'm a full-time theologian but also a full-time chauffeur. And when they are in the game, there's no place I'd rather be than with them.

In the very opening pages of Genesis, we have a similar picture of God the Father's desire to be with His children and walk with them in Eden. Though we've already looked at the story of Adam and Eve in this study, today, we'll look at a different idea regarding the Garden of Eden. Before there was the temple or a church, Eden was the meeting place where people encountered the presence of God.

01   Pause for a moment to think about God's physical presence in the Garden of Eden. What new insight or perspective on Genesis 1–3 comes to mind?

After the fall, God still longed to be near His people, but sin created a barrier. So God established systems and structures that would allow His presence to be near His beloved children, reminding them of His holiness and call for them to pursue holiness

Let's look at two structures God established to be near His people.

First, we have the **tent of meeting,** or the **tabernacle.**

The tent of meeting, also known as the tabernacle, was almost like a "mobile temple." It was a portable housing for the Lord, revealing that God is not isolated to a specific geographic location and would journey with His people. Because the tabernacle was set in the middle of their camp, it was also a reminder of whose they were.

There was still the issue of a Holy God needing to cleanse the sins of the people. We see the beginning of a sacrificial system immediately following the disobedience of Adam and Eve, when an animal was killed to provide clothing (Genesis 3:21). Then, in Genesis 4, Cain and Abel offered a sacrifice to God. As the sacrificial system became more formalized, the tabernacle communicated the holiness of God and was a reminder to the people that their sins were costly and required a sacrifice through the shedding of an animal's blood.

It's here we see a glimpse of the coming Messiah, whose blood would cleanse the sins of the people perfectly and permanently.

02   Read Exodus 25:8 and Numbers 35:34. What does God promise to do?

Within the tabernacle we also find elements pointing to Jesus. In the Holy Place, there was the Bread of Presence (representing the fact that God would always be a provider for Israel) and the Altar of Incense (representing light). Inside of the Holy of Holies, there was also the Ark of the Covenant (representing the presence of God). These images point to Jesus. Jesus is the sacrificial Bread and the Light of the World. And we no longer need the Ark of the Covenant because Jesus came down to earth and we can experience His presence for ourselves.

After the tabernacle, **the temple** came next.

When the Israelites settled in the promised land they were in a position to build a permanent structure. King David desired to build a temple for God, but his son Solomon eventually constructed it (2nd Samuel 7:1–15). Solomon's temple (1 Kings 6) was the grandest expression of the presence or "with-ness" of God.

Yet the temple, even in all its glory and grandeur, would eventually be destroyed. But through these transitions, we can pause to remember what made these places so special and significant to begin with . . . the very presence and promise of God's nearness.

The New Testament teaches there is no longer a need for a temple, because anyone who places their faith in Jesus actually becomes the new temple. This is Paul's emphatic statement in Ephesians 2. Through Jesus, the people of God become the new temple of God where the Spirit of Christ both "dwells" in and "indwells" the believer.

03   Read Ephesians 2:19–22. What stands out to you in these verses after learning more about the purposes of the tabernacle and the temple?

Let's return to the tabernacle for another connection to Jesus. The Hebrew word for tabernacle *(mishkan)* comes from the root of the Hebrew verb *shakan,* which means "to dwell" (Exodus 25:8). Later in the New Testament, John tells us Jesus came to "dwell" among us in John 1:14. The Greek word for "dwelled," *eskēnōsen,* is related to the Greek word *skēnē,* which means a "tent."

"And the Word became flesh and dwelt among us, and we have seen his glory, glory as of the only Son from the Father, full of grace and truth" (John 1:14).

John 1:14 tells us Jesus came and set up His tent, His place of dwelling, amongst humanity. Which in itself is mind-blowing, considering the sacredness surrounding the presence of God. Jesus is the fulfillment and tangible evidence of *dwelling* in John 1:14 that is originally rooted in these Old Testament passages.

Jesus is the "tent" God established. So what does this mean for us? There are two thoughts we want to leave you with as we close our first day of this study on presence this week:

THE PEOPLE OF THE OLD TESTAMENT HAD TO ENTER A PHYSICAL PLACE TO ENCOUNTER THE PRESENCE OF GOD UNTIL JESUS HIMSELF CAME TO US.

04   Read Matthew 1:23. Who is Jesus referred to as?

SINCE WE ARE NOW CONSIDERED GOD'S TEMPLE, HE HAS GIVEN US INSTRUCTIONS FOR HOLY LIVING.

05   Read 1 Corinthians 3:16, 17; 6:12–20; and 1 Peter 2:4–5. Jot down some takeaways that stand out to you as you reflect on being the new temple.

The presence of God came down through the miracle of Jesus and we are forever changed because of it. Friend, let's continue to look for Jesus in Scripture in the rest of our final week together!

Jacob's Ladder

GENESIS 28:10–15 / JOHN 1:51

Father, I desire that they also, whom you have given me, may be with me where I am, to see
my glory that you have given me because you loved me before the foundation of the world.

JOHN 17:24

The story of Jacob is evidence that God sometimes chooses the most unlikely people and imperfect families for key roles in His plans.

It's encouraging to know that broken relationships don't mean disqualification from ministry. God looks past the surface, past confusing pain, past questionable motives, and sees potential.

What good news for each of us today! God doesn't give up on us when He sees an area of weakness. In fact, sometimes our weakest areas, the areas that lead us into our deepest sorrow or even regret, when submitted humbly to God can be refined and guided into areas of beautiful strength.

Does God use imperfect people? Does God use families that have dysfunction? The answer is a resounding YES!

We will see this as we look deeper into the life of Jacob. For context, Jacob is the son of Isaac and Rebekah, and the grandson of Abraham. In his early years, he's a spoiled and favored baby boy, who develops some patterns of cheating and lying as a young man. However, God interacts personally with him in spite of his faults, and Jacob's life changes. Eventually, he learns to trust God in his darkest and most challenging moments. As a result, Jacob will be forever remembered as one of the "patriarchs" of the people of God.

One of the disturbing stories of Jacob is about him cheating his brother Esau out of his birthright (Genesis 27:41–44). He leaves home to get away from his brother, and heads to his Uncle Laban's home. One night, God gave Jacob a dream.

Read Genesis 28:10–15.

When we look at the Hebrew text and context, it's better to see this "ladder" more as a staircase. In the Ancient Near East, there would have been stone staircases that were built on ancient temple structures called "ziggurats." The ziggurat was a temple tower and it was believed that the staircase would be used by the divine to create access from the heavenly realm to the earthly realm.

What Jacob sees is essentially a staircase connecting heaven and earth.

Read Genesis 28:13. (*Hint: If your Bible has a little footnote or clarification for this verse, be sure and read it!)

In Genesis 28:13, many English translations say the Lord was standing above the ladder/staircase. But the Hebrew language states the Lord was standing beside the ladder. This spatial proximity is important because the Lord standing beside the ladder places Him near Jacob, not separated in the heavens.

01   Read Genesis 28:14–15. What does God promise Jacob?

This promise that God will be with His people will be a repeated phrase and concept. We saw it yesterday with the tent of the meeting/tabernacle and the temple. But now, we can see its deeper meaning in terms of personal relationship with His people.

The "with-ness" of God would follow Jacob everywhere. We can look at this promise from God for Jacob and know that God's nearness and presence was a right-now, present promise. But Jacob's story isn't the only one where we find this "with us" statement.

Look at the following verses and underline the common phrase:

ABRAHAM

At that time Abimelech and Phicol the commander of his army
said to Abraham, "God is with you in all that you do."

GENESIS 21:22

ISAAC

And the LORD appeared to him the same night and said, "I am the God of Abraham
your father. Fear not, for I am with you and will bless you and multiply your offspring
for my servant Abraham's sake."

GENESIS 26:24

JACOB

Behold, I am with you and will keep you wherever you go, and will bring you back to this land.
For I will not leave you until I have done what I have promised you.

GENESIS 28:15

JOSEPH

The LORD was with Joseph, and he became a successful man,
and he was in the house of his Egyptian master.

GENESIS 39:2

MOSES

He said, "But I will be with you, and this shall be the sign for you, that I have sent you:
when you have brought the people out of Egypt, you shall serve God on this mountain."

EXODUS 3:12

JOSHUA

No man shall be able to stand before you all the days of your life. Just as I was with Moses, so I will be
with you. I will not leave you or forsake you. Have I not commanded you? Be strong and courageous.
Do not be frightened, and do not be dismayed, for the LORD your God is with you wherever you go.

JOSHUA 1:5; JOSHUA 1:9

DAVID

And Nathan said to the king, "Go, do all that is in your heart, for the LORD is with you."

2 SAMUEL 7:3

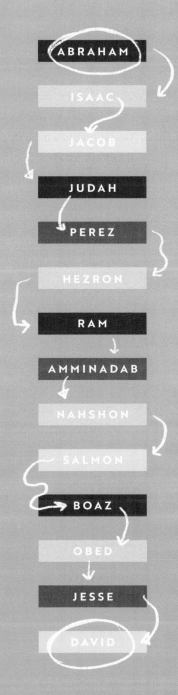

Lineage of Jacob

All the expectations of the Old Testament are found complete in Christ. In fact, we actually find out something even more important about the "with us" promise of the Lord, especially as it relates to the dream of the staircase.

02 Read John 1:51. What connection do you see to the ladder/staircase?

In John 1:51, Jesus is referring back to Genesis 28:12. The eight consecutive words in Greek (*"the angels of God ascending and descending on"*) correlate specifically to the language of Genesis 28:12.

And Jesus uses His words very carefully. In Jacob's dream, the angels ascended and descended on the staircase. And, the Lord was next to the staircase with a promise to be with Jacob. Now, Jesus declares that the staircase is in fact the *"Son of Man"* (John 1:51). Jesus is literally saying that He is the staircase.

This staircase connects heaven and earth, and Jesus is the way across. You see, the gap between heaven and earth prior to Jesus was the dark hole of sin and death. But through His sacrifice on the cross, Jesus becomes the staircase that connects heaven and earth for all those who would put their faith and trust in Him.

03 How does this imagery make you think differently about what it means to walk with Jesus?

Now read John 12:32.

In Jacob's dream, the emphasis was on the nearness of God. But as we look at Jesus in light of Jacob's dream, we see . . .

Jesus enters into human history by descending from heaven.

JOHN 3:13; JOHN 6:62

Jesus was physically and truly *with* His disciples.

JOHN 14:9; JOHN 14:25; JOHN 17:12

Jesus wants His believers to ascend to heaven to be with Him forever.

JOHN 17:24

The "with us" statements we read earlier recorded the promises God made to His people to always be with them. And, these promises are still true for us today in the life of Jesus.

We don't have to wait until the distant future. We can experience the presence of Jesus with us today through the Holy Spirit, who indwells the believers of Jesus (John 14:16).

Friend, wherever you are right now, take a moment and simply pray this prayer of thanks and gratitude to Jesus: "Jesus, thank You for being *with* me right now."

Pillar of Fire and Cloud of Smoke

EXODUS 13 / JOHN 8:12–30

Again Jesus spoke to them, saying, "I am the light of the world.
Whoever follows me will not walk in darkness, but will have the light of life."

JOHN 8:12

Do you remember traveling on a road trip before using a map app on your phone?

If you can, there's a high possibility you remember the days of printing turn-by-turn directions from MapQuest.com. Or before that, buying a printed road map or atlas! Oh, how far we've come!

Getting lost, missing exits, getting turned around . . . the confusion can leave us feeling so vulnerable.

It's incredibly dysregulating and sometimes downright frightening to be lost. The Israelites most definitely felt this vulnerability and anxiety when they left Egypt. Yes, they were leaving the devastating hardships of Egypt, but every step took them deeper into the unknown. And the unknown can be a frightening place to willingly walk into.

God . . . where am I supposed to be going?

From the start of the Israelites' exit from Egypt, God kept His promise not just to lead His people, but to be with them every step of the way.

01   Read Exodus 13:17–18a. Take note of the words in verse 18a, especially *"But God led the people around by the way of the wilderness toward the Red Sea."* How does it make you feel, reading that God intentionally led the Israelites *into* the wilderness?

It's hard to understand why God would intentionally take the Israelites through such a desolate place like the wilderness. Maybe today you find yourself questioning God in a place you find yourself in.

God . . . *why am I here?*
God . . . *where are You?*
God . . . *what am I supposed to be doing?*
God . . . *where am I supposed to be going?*

The wilderness wasn't God's punishment because He didn't care. It was where God took them because He knew something they didn't.

God knew going the shorter journey through the land of the Philistines was a greater danger to them in the long run. If the Israelites faced the Philistines, their fear might have prompted them to turn back to Egypt. Or, they might have been tempted by the idolatry of the Philistines and turn towards false gods.

God was not unaware of the needs of the Israelites. And God is not unaware of your deepest needs. The promise of God's presence would carry the Israelites through what appeared to be their worst nightmare in the wilderness.

02   Read Exodus 13:21–22. What was the manifestation of God's presence that went before them?

These manifestations served two important purposes:

. . . **The pillars led the people in the direction that they should go.**
. . . **The pillars provided boundaries and protection for the people.**

Let's zoom in on the image here. The Israelites saw the tangible presence of God leading and guiding them day and night. Even though the Israelites cried out in complaints and weariness from the journey that felt purposeless to them, God's presence continued to guide them.

Here is one of the challenges we face when experiencing unexpected pain and suffering: We can believe there is an underlying meaninglessness to what we're facing. But through uncovering these details within the story of Israel in the wilderness, we see there is not a single moment of our hardship and hurt that is not used by God to bring forth a greater good and purpose.

The question isn't so much about the direction in which God is leading us—it's about our *obedience* along the way.

03   Think about where you are today. What might obedience to God look like here?

The pillar of cloud by day and pillar of fire by night didn't just lead God's people; it also served as a protective boundary.

The people always knew how far ahead they could go. This clear boundary gave them a visible marking of what *too far* would be. Too far would simply be to step in front of the pillar of cloud or fire, putting them outside or ahead of the presence of God and the pace of His leading.

04   Have you experienced the Lord leading you or revealing a boundary to you? What did that look like?

The best place for us to follow is in God's direction, and at His pace. Wherever He is leading, His presence and protection is coming with Him. The wilderness wasn't strong enough to strip that away. And whatever you're facing right now isn't either.

What the pillar of cloud by day and pillar of fire by night did for the Israelites in the wilderness, Jesus does in completion and fulfillment for all those who believe in Him. To close today, let's look specifically at these connections to Jesus:

Jesus is "the light of the world."

JOHN 8:12

When Jesus says He is the *"light of the world"* in John 8:12, it is a promise of orientation and direction. Just like the pillar of cloud by day and pillar of fire by night provided direction for the Israelites, we have this same guide in the person of Jesus.

In the darkest moments of our life, when we feel unseen, disregarded or abandoned, we can remember that the Light shines in the darkness, and the darkness cannot overcome it (John 1:5). Wherever the Light of Christ is, there is hope. This isn't just a good-sounding Christian slogan. This is truth. And sometimes it's helpful to speak this out loud over whatever you are facing. Remember, lies flee in the presence of truth, just like darkness flees in the presence of light.

Jesus is "the way, and the truth, and the life."

JOHN 14:6

Where there is the light, there is the promise of life. John 1:4 says, *"In him was life, and the life was the light of men."* In Jesus, we find the life all of humanity longs for. And we can also be assured that Jesus will guide us along our way through the Truth of His Word and His presence.

Jesus is the "good shepherd" who promises to lead His people.

JOHN 10:11; JOHN 10:27

Sheep depend on the care and protection of a shepherd, and we can depend on the care of Jesus as our Good Shepherd. Read the words of Jesus in John 10:27–28: *"My sheep hear my voice, and I know them, and they follow me. I give them eternal life, and they will never perish, and no one will snatch them out of my hand."*

This takes some humility to lean into His guidance, but we also need to grow attuned to the voice of Jesus so we can obey when He is speaking to us. In the hard, desolate places in our lives, it can feel like Jesus is absent. But if we take a moment to pause, be silent, watch, and really listen, we can both see the light of His presence and hear the comfort of His voice.

God's presence never departed from the Israelites, and Jesus is with us even now. We pray today that you found yourself comforted and cared for even in the hardest place you could find yourself in.

Take heart, friend. He is with you.

Angel of the Lord

EXODUS 3:1–6 / JOHN 14:15–27

———

Jesus replied, "Anyone who loves me will obey my teaching. My Father
will love them, and we will come to them and make our home with them."

JOHN 14:23 NIV

As we've discovered Jesus in the Scripture through the lens of *presence* this week, here are some key words from what we've studied so far about God's presence:

Closeness

Proximity

Guidance

Protection

Access

Relationship

Through reading the Old Testament, we see Jesus is pre-existing. Which simply means Jesus was in the beginning with God the Father and God the Spirit, but He was not yet in bodily form. We refer to this as "pre-incarnate Jesus"—Jesus in His "pre-bodily" form. This is what makes the mystery of what we've been studying so intriguing and profound. Jesus was spiritually present before He was physically present.

01   What has been one of your biggest takeaways in this study? Have you experienced Jesus in a new way?

Jesus wasn't in hiding before He came to earth in the flesh. Today we will see in passages of Scripture that Jesus was active, specifically that Jesus is the angel of the Lord and the commander of the Lord's army.

The angel of the Lord first makes an appearance in an odd place: in the middle of a bush, speaking to Moses. We tend to read this story and understand that Moses is talking to God. But there's a significant detail in the story that can easily be overlooked.

02   Read Exodus 3:2. Who does the text say appeared to Moses?

The phrase "out of the midst" comes from a Hebrew word that can just be translated "middle." The angel of the Lord was actually in the bush, and since we're told "God" called to Moses from the bush (Exodus 3:4), God's voice is connected with the angel of the Lord.

But there's more . . . read Exodus 3:3–5.

03   What is Moses instructed to do?

The angel of the Lord is in the bush and the text says that the Lord calls out of the bush, so we can conclude that the angel of the Lord is that voice calling out of the bush. This by itself is incredibly important, but there's even more detail to unpack!

When Moses is told to take off his sandals because the place he's standing is holy ground (Exodus 3:5), what does this actually imply? Think about our study earlier this week on the tabernacle and the temple and what made those places holy: the presence of the Lord. So we can be confident the Lord was in fact present with Moses. But here, the presence of the Lord and His voice is connected to the presence of the angel of the Lord. This would lead us to believe that the angel of the Lord and the Lord Himself are one and the same. Think about it like the Trinity. They are all the same in essence yet distinct in person.

Let's keep digging. The burning bush is not the only time where someone is told to take off their sandals in the presence of a heavenly messenger. Turn to read Joshua 5:15.

04   What is Joshua told to do?

IN THIS PASSAGE JOSHUA IS MET BY "THE COMMANDER OF THE LORD'S ARMY" (JOSHUA 5:15). THERE'S GOOD REASON TO CONNECT THIS "COMMANDER" WITH THE "ANGEL OF THE LORD" (V. 2) IN EXODUS 3:2–5. WE CAN DRAW THE CONCLUSION THAT THIS IS NOT JUST AN ARBITRARY MESSENGER BUT THE DIVINE PRESENCE OF GOD HIMSELF. HERE IS HOW:

Moses and Joshua both worship in the presence of the angel.

In Scripture there is never another example of an angel accepting human worship. This would have been idolatry (Exodus 20; Deuteronomy 5–8).

The *holiness* associated with the space where the angel presents himself indicates *sacred* space.

We can connect this back to the temple and the Holy of Holies because the presence of God was there.

In Joshua 6 the story continues and there is a *blending* of the angel and God Himself.

The events that take place in Exodus 3:2–5, with the angel of the Lord speaking with the voice of God, are the same events that progress with Joshua.

The evidence seems to tell us that the *"angel of the Lord"* (Exodus 3:2) and the *"commander of the Lord's army"* (Joshua 5:15) are none other than the "direct representative of Yahweh or the embodiment of Yahweh in human or angelic form." Even more simply put: the pre-incarnate Jesus.

Jesus was in the beginning with God the Father and God the Spirit, and was not yet in bodily form. Jesus has been with God's people throughout the events recorded in the Old Testament from the very beginning.

Within our Bibles we have an exciting truth revealed to us: The man who walked the earth 2,000 years ago, whom we call Jesus, is actually God the Son, and has been walking the earth and leading His people to Him and His Kingdom from the very beginning of time. He has never been limited to the time period He physically walked the earth.

Hear Jesus' own words about His history: *"So the Jews said to him, 'You are not yet fifty years old, and have you seen Abraham?' Jesus said to them, 'Truly, truly, I say to you, before Abraham was, I am'"* (John 8:57–58).

As I studied all that is in today's teaching, I literally wanted to weep. Partly because I've so desperately wanted burning bush experiences where the Lord spoke so clearly to me. And partly because I've also wanted a divine messenger to appear before me and speak audibly.

But as we've gone through this day, I have realized, Jesus has been speaking to me directly through the Bible and through discernment that comes from the Holy Spirit so much more than I've realized. Read what Jesus promised to His disciples and us, too:

"All this I have spoken while still with you. But the Advocate, the Holy Spirit, whom the Father will send in my name, will teach you all things and will remind you of everything I have said to you. Peace I leave with you; my peace I give you. I do not give to you as the world gives. Do not let your hearts be troubled and do not be afraid" (John 14:25–27 NIV).

I want to start taking off my shoes to mark my time in reading the Bible and in prayer as holy moments because the presence of the Lord is there, guiding me, speaking to me. And that is just too incredible to not fully acknowledge.

In the days of the tabernacle and temple, very few ever got to actually go into the holy of holies. But for you and me, this can be an everyday reality if we choose it.

Friend, we only have one more day of study together. Let's ask the Lord to continue to reveal Himself to us.

The Incarnation

LUKE 2

But the angel said to them, "Do not be afraid. I bring you good news that will cause great joy for all the people. Today in the town of David a Savior has been born to you; he is the Messiah, the Lord."

LUKE 2:10–11 NIV

One of the hardest scenarios to process as a human is when we've been looking forward to something and it falls apart.

We wait in eager anticipation for it . . .
We tell our friends about it . . .
We dream about the fulfillment of it . . .

And the moment that it all comes crashing down is devastating.

Maybe it was something you were dreaming up on your own. Or maybe it was a promise made to you by someone else they didn't keep.

Broken promises and broken dreams lead to broken pieces of our heart.

What a tragedy it would be if all the events and promises in the Old Testament of the coming Messiah never took place. What an immense heartbreak if we opened our Bibles and in the table of contents we only had the Old Testament but not the New Testament. But because of God's faithfulness, none of these hypothetical heartbreaks are true. And as we've journeyed through the Old Testament looking for Jesus, we've seen rich evidence over and over again of just how very present Jesus was and is. He's never been absent.

The Messiah, the Anointed One, was present at every turn of every page in the Old Testament in so many different ways.

01   Think back on all you've learned about Jesus these past six weeks. How do these truths encourage your heart in places you may feel disappointed or disillusioned today?

02   How do these truths challenge you to look at something you're facing with more assurance that the Lord is with you?

For such a long-awaited moment in human history, we may expect the most glorious, highly produced, red-carpet entrance. The most spectacular palace filled with the largest banquet of food and drink. And maybe some orchestra music and a choir singing His praises as He's so warmly welcomed.

This is what we would expect. In fact, this is exactly what the wise men expected when they saw a sign in the heavens that told of the birth of a new King. This is exactly why the wise men's first stop was King Herod's palace (Matthew 2:1–3).

Where else would a future king be born but in a palace?

But King Herod's palace was empty, and the King of heaven and earth instead was born in the most unforeseen place: *a barn.*

Before we continue studying the incarnation and birth of Jesus, there is some historical background information that's important for us to grasp.

The emperor of Rome at the time was Augustus, and he was known as the one who brought peace to Rome. In fact, Augustus was such a big deal that he was seen as the hope of the world at the time. We can know this because various historians have noted how:

- THE EMPIRE CELEBRATED HIM.
- CHOIRS IN THE PALACE SANG HIS PRAISES.
- HE WAS VIEWED AS A GOD.
- HE WAS THOUGHT TO HAVE SAVED ROME.
- HE ALLEGEDLY BROUGHT PEACE.
- HE PROVED HE HAD POWER BY TAXING THE PEOPLE.

Luke is such a brilliant historian in the way he details the birth of Jesus in Luke 2. It's intentionally designed to help us see how Jesus, in a peculiar way, surpasses everything that Augustus accomplished. But Jesus does this through the most unorthodox ways.

- HE WAS BORN IN HUMBLE CIRCUMSTANCES, YET ALL OF CREATION CELEBRATES HIM.
- HE HAD NO EARTHLY PALACE, YET ANGELS SING HIS PRAISES.
- SOME DENIED HIS DIVINITY, BUT JESUS IS GOD.
- THROUGH SELF-SACRIFICE, JESUS SAVED NOT ONLY ROME BUT THE ENTIRE WORLD.
- JESUS DID NOT FOCUS ON POLITICAL PEACEMAKING BUT BROUGHT A MORE IMPORTANT SPIRITUAL PEACE.
- JESUS PROVED HIS POWER NOT BY EXERTING HIS AUTHORITY AND CAUSING OTHERS TO SUFFER (LIKE AUGUSTUS' TAXES) BUT BY LAYING HIS OWN LIFE DOWN AND SUFFERING ON THE CROSS.

Augustus	Jesus
THE EMPIRE CELEBRATED HIM.	HE WAS BORN IN HUMBLE CIRCUMSTANCES, YET ALL OF CREATION CELEBRATES HIM.
CHOIRS IN THE PALACE SANG HIS PRAISES.	HE HAD NO EARTHLY PALACE, YET ANGELS SING HIS PRAISES.
HE WAS VIEWED AS A GOD.	SOME DENIED HIS DIVINITY, BUT JESUS *IS* GOD.
HE WAS THOUGHT TO HAVE SAVED ROME.	THROUGH SELF-SACRIFICE, JESUS SAVED NOT ONLY ROME BUT THE ENTIRE WORLD.
HE ALLEGEDLY BROUGHT PEACE.	JESUS DID NOT FOCUS ON POLITICAL PEACEMAKING BUT BROUGHT A MORE IMPORTANT SPIRITUAL PEACE.
HE PROVED HE HAD POWER BY TAXING THE PEOPLE.	JESUS PROVED HIS POWER NOT BY EXERTING HIS POWER AND CAUSING OTHERS TO SUFFER (LIKE AUGUSTUS' TAXES) BUT BY LAYING HIS OWN LIFE DOWN AND SUFFERING ON THE CROSS.

03   What stands out to you the most as you see the comparison between Augustus and Jesus?

You see, if we expected Jesus to come as a triumphant earthly king and behave in the same way as Augustus, we would have absolutely missed Him. We would have been disappointed, confused, and grown even more weary over time that God was just getting our hopes up. In fact, we probably would have believed that Jesus never even showed up. It would have left us empty and even defeated.

04   How does it encourage you that every single promise of the coming Messiah was fulfilled through Jesus?

The greatest miracle of all is not just that Jesus came . . . but that He came down from heaven to take on human flesh to be with us. He could have come in so many other ways that were grander, less every day, and certainly in ways that required much less suffering on his part. But he didn't choose that. Instead, he came to be with us and suffer alongside us.

05   Take a moment to close today and thank God for sending Jesus to earth and how present
     he has been and will forever be with you. Jot down some final takeaways from this week.

Well, friend, here we are. The last lap.

We hope you learned so much over the last six weeks as we've gotten into God's Word and let God's
Word get into us.

But we hope you learned more than a few new facts. We pray that, as you saw Jesus in the hidden places
of these Old Testament Scriptures, it stirred your faith to look for Him in whatever you're facing in
your life today.

Conclusion

A couple of years ago, I wrote this in my journal:

Jesus told us we would have trouble in this world but then encouraged us to take heart because He'd overcome the world. So why doesn't it feel like He is overcoming the heartbreaking realities in my world? I was facing so much grief and uncertainty. It seemed some of my favorite parts of my life were unraveling. Nothing was making sense. And just when I thought I could see a light at the end of the tunnel, more hard things hit me.

I got angry at Him.

I wrestled and cried and tried with everything in me to figure things out on my own.

But the more I tried to untangle the mess, the bigger it seemed to get. Nothing was working.
Nothing at all was working.

So I knew I had a choice to make. I could either believe that Jesus was with me or get completely swallowed up in all the confusion and pain, believing Jesus had abandoned me. Whatever I chose to focus on is what would be magnified in my life. And I certainly didn't want my problems and pain to get any more magnified. So I started making the choice daily to intentionally declare over my problems that somehow walking through this was going to help me see Jesus more clearly. And it did.

The problems didn't go away. But my courage to face them came back stronger than ever. Knowing I wasn't in this battle alone helped me start believing that Jesus would help me eventually overcome, and I learned so much more about Him in the process. We won't see Him unless we are intentionally seeking and looking.

Now, as we wrap up this study, I think it's time to add a few more lines to that journal entry:

Just because we can't always see Jesus doesn't mean He isn't there.
Just because we aren't hearing Him doesn't mean He's being silent.

I know we've said this in different ways all throughout this study. But maybe you need to read those last two sentences over and over as much as I do.

When the circumstances we face feel crushing, scary, confusing or truly just impossible to figure out, how can we know that Jesus really is with us?

After six weeks in this study we hope you can now respond to this question with more assurance of this answer: Because He always has been. And it's more than a promise for the future. It's a reality right now. Jesus is actively with us.

A significant takeaway from this whole study for me has been that if we can see Jesus' presence in the Old Testament then we can have more confidence and assurance He is present in our lives right now, too.

It's surprising how explicit the New Testament authors are about Jesus' presence in the Old Testament:

- The "I Am" in whom Abraham rejoiced was Jesus (John 8:56–58).
- The Lord who motivated Moses was Christ (Hebrews 11:26).
- The Redeemer who brought God's people out of Egypt was Jesus (Jude 5).
- The Rock in the wilderness was Christ (1 Corinthians 10:4).
- The King of Isaiah's temple vision was the Son (John 12:40–41).

Jesus is not merely patterned, pointed to, and promised in the Old Testament; He is present.

Jesus is God's best kept promise. And He hand-delivered that kept promise to earth for us. Look at these instances within the Old Testament that show us God came down to us:

GENESIS 3:8–9

God came down into the Garden of Eden and sought after Adam and Eve as they hid themselves. God sent them out of Eden not purely punitively but in a way laced with mercy and grace, so they would not live in eternal separation from God.

GENESIS 11:7

God came down to observe the people He created in His likeness and image, who had sinned against Him in an act of full-on rebellion. Rather than going out into the world to multiply the image of God and making His name great, as they were commanded (Genesis 1:28; Genesis 9:1; Genesis 9:7), they decided to reach up into the heavens to make a name for themselves. God diversified their tongues so that they would still spread out and multiply. Another consequence laced with mercy and grace.

GENESIS 18:20–21

God came down—He saw and He Heard. The outcry against Sodom and Gomorrah was great, and the cries reached God. God wouldn't sit back like an absentee father. No, He investigated the claims, and after His investigation, He acted. And while the city received judgment (justice) in response to overwhelming sin, God still showed mercy and grace by saving Lot and his daughters.

God. Came. Down. And every time, He acted. Through the chaos of rebellion and sin, He continued to act in mercy and grace.

And there's no greater act of God coming down than when He appeared in human history, as recorded in Matthew 1:1.

All the promises of God's presence with us come into fulfillment in the birth of Jesus. And theologically this is referred to as the "incarnation," when God entered human history by taking on human flesh, remaining 100% God and 100% man all at the same time. Theologian Karl Barth said this of Jesus: "This man is the secret of heaven and earth, of the cosmos created by God."[42]

As we reflect on the last six weeks we can remind ourselves that Jesus wasn't absent but that people were looking in all the wrong places.

The incarnation of Christ is a reminder to us all that not a single promise present in the Old Testament was left unfulfilled. C.S Lewis may have said it best: "The Son of God became a man to enable men to become sons of God."[43] Every single promise of the coming Messiah in the Old Testament came to fruition in the middle of the night in a manger in Bethlehem. Jesus

had arrived. He just happened to make His entry in the most unexpected way.

And the same is true in our life right now. He is present. Jesus is never hiding from us. He's waiting to be seen by us.

In the hard places.
In the hurting places.
In the not-yet-healed places.
In the uncertain places.
In the waiting places.
In the celebrating places.
And especially in the everyday places.

We pray you see Jesus.

In the beginning of this study, we shared this truth with you:

Jesus is never absent in the story of the Bible, and He's certainly not absent in any part of our story either.

And we want to remind you of this truth as we bring our time together to a close . . . Jesus is our reminder that God always keeps His promises. But if we don't know His promise-filled words, we won't know what to remember. John 8:32 says, "you will know the truth, and the truth will set you free." The only truth that sets us free is the truth we know. This is why it's so important to study Scripture because it's the only thing that will lead to freedom.

My opinion will never set me free.
My grace to others will never
set me free.
My generosity will never set me free.
My trying to be good enough will
never set me free.

If we really want to walk in freedom, we have to remember God is who He says He is and believe with every ounce of faith in our hearts that He really does keep His word. It is the Truth of God that will set us free and keep us from being entrapped by the deceiving lies in our head. Our enemy will sometimes bombard us with harsh comments trying to get us to believe God has forgotten us. But that's when we want you to remember this study. Pull it back down off your shelf and revisit all we've learned during this time together. We promise, we will need to do the very same thing.

So don't stop here. Keep diving into Scripture, learning and looking and seeking more Truth-filled words from God. And when you do, don't forget to look up and see Jesus. Because, from cover to cover, He's there.

He's never been absent. We've never been left alone.

And even better . . . He's returning soon (Revelation 22:12–20). We are held safe in the embrace of a God who promises the comfort of His presence from the garden to glory.

God, thank You that Your Word is so applicable. Lord, help us to remember the Truth we've discovered in Your Word together. We love You so much, God. We make a commitment today to start really paying attention and looking for Jesus in the unexpected places of our lives. In Jesus' Name, Amen.

He's **never** been absent. **We've** never **been** left alone.

A Guided Prayer To Receive Salvation

Hi friend,

When I was in my early 20s, I felt very distant from God. A series of heartbreaking situations in my life made me question His goodness and whether or not He really loved me. But through His divine grace, eventually Truth broke through my cold resistance and brought me to the place where I wanted to accept His love and dedicate my life to Him. The challenge was that I didn't know how to do this and I was too afraid to ask my friends. As I remember struggling through this years ago, I wonder if you might be facing this same struggle, too. Maybe you've had some ups and downs with this whole God thing, but finally you're in a place where you want to give your heart to Him, accept His grace, and receive salvation. If that's you, I'd like to invite you to pray this salvation prayer with me today:

Dear God, thank You for the gifts of grace and forgiveness. Thank You that, in the midst of my sin, You have made a way, through Jesus, to forgive my sin and make me right with You. So today I confess my sinfulness . . . my hard heart . . . my mean thoughts . . . my harsh words . . . my doubt. I believe with all my heart that it was for me—and because of me—that Jesus died. Please forgive me of all my sin. Big sins. Small sins. Past sins. Present sins. And all sins to come. I exchange my sin for Jesus' goodness and holiness. By the shed blood of Jesus, I am now forgiven and free! Thank You that, in this moment, You have sealed me with Your Holy Spirit. I receive this precious gift and trust You will do as You promise and make me a new creation, molding and shaping me from the inside out to be more like You! I celebrate that the old me is gone and the new me is here to stay! I love You and am forever grateful for Your forgiveness and my new life in You. I ask all this in Jesus' name. Amen.

I love you, dear friend. And I'm rejoicing with all of heaven over every decision made to accept God's free gift of salvation. It truly is the sweetest gift we'll ever receive.

Love,
Lysa TerKeurst

Notes

Notes

Notes

Notes

Notes

Correlations Between OT and NT in Micah 5:2-6

	OT CORRELATIONS	NT CORRELATIONS
5:2[1] Will come out of Bethlehem	Jer 23:5 (Jer 30:21)	Matt 2:6; Luke 2:15; John 7:42
5:2[1] Ruler in Israel	Isa 9:6–7; Jer 30:21; 34:5	Matt 27:11; Heb 1:3
5:2[1] His origin is from before the days of old		John 1:1–3; 17:5; 1 John 1:1
5:3[2] Will instigate a return of Israel	Isa 11:11–12; 49:5–6; Mic 7:14	Acts 1:6–7
5:4[3] Stand and shepherd	Isa 11:3; 40:11; 42:1; Jer 23:4–6	John 10:11; Heb 13:20; 1 Pet 5:4; Rev 7:17
5:4[3] In the strength and majesty of Yahweh	Isa 49:3, 5; 60:21	John 14:10; Heb 13:20
5:4[3] He will be magnified in the earth	Ps 110; Isa 9:6; 52:13	John 17:5; Acts 19:17; Heb 1:3; 8:1; 2 Pet 1:16
5:5[4] He will be Peace	Isa 9:6; 11:6–9	Eph 2:14; Col 1:20
5:6[5] Shepherd with a sword	Isa 9:4–5; 49:2	Matt 10:34; Rev 1:16; 2:16; 19:15

1.   In Matthew 1:21–23 the name "Yeshua" means "God will save His people from sins." As NT scholar Patrick Schreiner says, "The saving from sins is a distinctly priestly task." Additionally, Jesus begins his earthly ministry at 30, the same age priests would begin their priestly duties (Numbers 4:3, 23, 30, 35, 39, 43, 47; 1 Chronicles 23:3). The Kingship examples are based on the fact that Jesus is called "Son of David," a designation of royalty and kingship. Additionally, all of the Gospels declare that Jesus was the "King of the Jews" (Matthew 27:37; Mark 15:26; Luke 23:38; John 19:19). For more, see: Patrick Schreiner, *The Ascension of Christ: Recovering a Neglected Doctrine* (Lexham Press, 2020).

2.   G. K. Beale, *The Temple and the Church's Mission: A Biblical Theology of the Dwelling Place of God*, ed. D. A. Carson, vol. 17, New Studies in Biblical Theology (Downers Grove, IL; England: InterVarsity Press; Apollos, 2004), 81.

3.   William Lee Holladay and Ludwig Köhler, *A Concise Hebrew and Aramaic Lexicon of the Old Testament* (Leiden: Brill, 2000), 377.

4.   R. Kent Hughes, *Hebrews: An Anchor for the Soul, vol. 1, Preaching the Word* (Wheaton, IL: Crossway Books, 1993), 112.

5.   David Noel Freedman, Helmer Ringgren, and M. P. O'Connor, "יהוה," ed. G. Johannes Botterweck, trans. David E. Green, *Theological Dictionary of the Old Testament*, vol. 5 (Grand Rapids, MI; Cambridge, U.K.: William B. Eerdmans Publishing Company, 1986), 500.

6.   Discover the eight major things humanity longs for and how Jesus fulfills all of them for us in *"The Answers to Your Deepest Longings: 40 Days Through the Bible."* Purchase your copy at p31bookstore.com today!

7.   See 1 Kings 3:14; 9:4–5; 11:4–6, 31–34, 38; 14:7–8; 15:1–5, 11–15; 2 Kings 14:1–4; 16:1–3; 18:1–3; 22:1–2.

8.   Christopher J. H. Wright, *Knowing Jesus Through the Old Testament* (Downers Grove, IL: InterVarsity Press, 2014), 16.

9.   Derek Kidner, *Genesis: An Introduction and Commentary*, vol. 1, Tyndale Old Testament Commentaries (Downers Grove, IL: InterVarsity Press, 1967), 75.

10. Douglas Mangum, Miles Custis, and Wendy Widder, Genesis 1–11, *Lexham Research Commentaries* (Bellingham, WA: Lexham Press, 2012), Ge 3:1–24.

11. Harry A. Hoffner Jr., 1 & 2 Samuel, ed. H. Wayne House and William Barrick, *Evangelical Exegetical Commentary* (Bellingham, WA: Lexham Press, 2015), 1 Sa 2:1.

12. David Tsumura, The First Book of Samuel, *The New International Commentary on the Old Testament* (Grand Rapids, MI: Wm. B. Eerdmans Publishing Co., 2007), 142.

13. R. Bartelmus, "יהוה," ed. G. Johannes Botterweck, Helmer Ringgren, and Heinz-Josef Fabry, trans. David E. Green, *Theological Dictionary of the Old Testament*, vol. 13 (Grand Rapids, MI; Cambridge, U.K.: William B. Eerdmans Publishing Company, 2004), 431.

14. M. G. Easton, *Easton's Bible Dictionary* (New York: Harper & Brothers, 1893).

15. Peter C. Craigie, Psalms 1–50, 2nd ed., vol. 19, *Word Biblical Commentary* (Nashville, TN: Nelson Reference & Electronic, 2004), 68.

16. Kenneth L. Barker, Micah, Nahum, Habakkuk, Zephaniah, vol. 20, *The New American Commentary* (Nashville: Broadman & Holman Publishers, 1999), 95.

17. Hans-Jürgen Zobel, "שֵׁבֶט," ed. G. Johannes Botterweck, Helmer Ringgren, and Heinz-Josef Fabry, trans. Douglas W. Stott, *Theological Dictionary of the Old Testament*, vol. 14 (Grand Rapids, MI; Cambridge, U.K.: William B. Eerdmans Publishing Company, 2004), 305.

18. JoAnna M. Hoyt, Amos, Jonah, & Micah, ed. H. Wayne House and William D. Barrick, *Evangelical Exegetical Commentary* (Bellingham, WA: Lexham Press, 2018), 727.

19. Harold G. Stigers, "1879 צֶדֶק," ed. R. Laird Harris, Gleason L. Archer Jr., and Bruce K. Waltke, *Theological Wordbook of the Old Testament* (Chicago: Moody Press, 1999), 752.

20. William Lee Holladay and Ludwig Köhler, *A Concise Hebrew and Aramaic Lexicon of the Old Testament* (Leiden: Brill, 2000), 221.

21. Translation taken from John Goldingay.

22. David Seal, "Satan," ed. John D. Barry et al., *The Lexham Bible Dictionary* (Bellingham, WA: Lexham Press, 2016).

23. M. Görg, "וחת," ed. G. Johannes Botterweck, Helmer Ringgren, and Heinz-Josef Fabry, trans. David E. Green, *Theological Dictionary of the Old Testament* (Grand Rapids, MI; Cambridge, U.K.: William B. Eerdmans Publishing Company, 2006), 565.

24. S. R. Driver, A Critical and Exegetical Commentary on Deuteronomy, 3rd ed., *International Critical Commentary* (Edinburgh: T. & T. Clark, 1902), 357.

25. William Lee Holladay and Ludwig Köhler, *A Concise Hebrew and Aramaic Lexicon of the Old Testament* (Leiden: Brill, 2000), 308.

26. JoAnna M. Hoyt, Amos, Jonah, & Micah, ed. H. Wayne House and William D. Barrick, *Evangelical Exegetical Commentary* (Bellingham, WA: Lexham Press, 2018), 728.

27. This quote is from Dr. N. T. Wright in his podcast *Ask N. T. Wright Anything*.

28. John H. Walton, "The Mesopotamian Background of the Tower of Babel Account and Its Implications," Bible and Spade 9, no. 3 (1996): 82.

29. Dane C. Ortlund, *Gentle and Lowly: The Heart of Christ for Sinners and Sufferers* (Wheaton, Ill: Crossway, 2020), 57.

30. Flavius Josephus and William Whiston, *The Works of Josephus: Complete and Unabridged* (Peabody: Hendrickson, 1987), 804.

31. Andrew T. Abernethy and Gregory Goswell, *God's Messiah in the Old Testament: Expectations of a Coming King* (Baker Academic, 2020), 58.

32. Grant R. Osborne, Matthew, vol. 1, *Zondervan Exegetical Commentary on the New Testament* (Grand Rapids, MI: Zondervan, 2010), 229.

33. Thomas R. Schreiner, Hebrews, ed. T. Desmond Alexander, Thomas R. Schreiner, and Andreas J. Köstenberger, *Evangelical Biblical Theology Commentary* (Bellingham, WA: Lexham Press, 2021), 164.

34. Eugene Carpenter, Exodus, ed. H. Wayne House and William D. Barrick, vol. 1, *Evangelical Exegetical Commentary* (Bellingham, WA: Lexham Press, 2012), 503.

35. Andrew Knowles, *The Bible Guide,* 1st Augsburg books ed. (Minneapolis, MN: Augsburg, 2001), 370.

36. Seth Postell, Eitan Bar, and Erez Soref, *Reading Moses, Seeing Jesus: How the Torah Fulfills Its Goal in Yeshua* (Bellingham, WA: Weaver Book Company, 2018),18.

37. Seth Postell, Eitan Bar, and Erez Soref, *Reading Moses, Seeing Jesus: How the Torah Fulfills Its Goal in Yeshua* (Bellingham, WA: Weaver Book Company, 2018), 94.

38. John Goldingay, A Critical and Exegetical Commentary on Isaiah 56–66, ed. G. I. Davies and C. M. Tuckett, *International Critical Commentary* (London; New Delhi; New York; Sydney: Bloomsbury, 2014), 221.

39. Andrew T. Abernethy, The Book of Isaiah and God's Kingdom: A Thematic—Theological Approach, ed. D. A. Carson, vol. 40, *New Studies in Biblical Theology* (Downers Grove, IL; London: Apollos; InterVarsity Press, 2016), 90.

40. John N. Oswalt, The Book of Isaiah, Chapters 40–66, *The New International Commentary on the Old Testament* (Grand Rapids, MI: Wm. B. Eerdmans Publishing Co., 1998), 527.

41. "https://www.desiringgod.org/articles/where-is-jesus-in-the-old-testament"

42. Karl Barth, Church Dogmatics III/1, *The Doctrine of Creation, Part 1,* ed. G. W. Bromiley and T. F. Torrance (Edinburgh: T&T Clark, 1958), p. 21.

43. C. S. Lewis, *Mere Christianity* (New York: HarperOne, 2001), 178.

Lysa TerKeurst

Lysa TerKeurst is president and chief visionary officer of Proverbs 31 Ministries and the author of six *New York Times* bestsellers, including *Good Boundaries and Goodbyes, Forgiving What You Can't Forget,* and *It's Not Supposed to Be This Way.* She writes from her family's farm table and lives in North Carolina. Connect with her at www.LysaTerKeurst.com or on social media @LysaTerKeurst.

Dr. Joel Muddamalle

Dr. Joel Muddamalle (PhD in Theology) is the Director of Theology and Research at Proverbs 31 Ministries and the theologian in residence for Haven Place Ministries, a ministry of Lysa TerKeurst, that provides personalized theology and therapy retreats and smaller gatherings. He also cohosts the popular podcast *Therapy and Theology* with Lysa and licensed counselor Jim Cress. Joel serves on the preaching team at Transformation Church with Pastor Derwin Gray and is a frequent speaker for conferences and events. Based in Charlotte, NC, Joel and his wife have four children and two dogs.

Proverbs 31
MINISTRIES

Know the Truth. Live the Truth. It changes everything.

If you were inspired by this *30 Days with Jesus* study and desire to deepen your own personal relationship with Jesus Christ, Proverbs 31 Ministries has just what you are looking for.

Proverbs 31 Ministries exists to be a trusted friend who will take you by the hand and walk by your side, leading you one step closer to the heart of God through:

- Free online daily devotions
- First 5 Bible study app
- Online Bible studies
- Podcast
- COMPEL writer training
- She Speaks Conference
- Books and resources

Our desire is to help you to know the Truth and live the Truth. Because when you do, it changes everything.

For more information about Proverbs 31 Ministries, visit: www.Proverbs31.org.

> *We must exchange whispers with God*
> *before shouts with the world.*

LYSA TERKEURST

THE
FIRST 5 MOBILE APP
BY PROVERBS 31 MINISTRIES!

Designed for you to spend the first five minutes
of your day reading and studying God's Word.

This free mobile app will take you through the
Bible chapter by chapter, with daily teachings
and weekend audio recordings to accompany
each passage of Scripture.

DOWNLOAD
from your smartphone app store!
WWW.FIRST5.ORG

MORE BIBLE STUDIES BY *Lysa TerKeurst*

Made to Crave

According to Lysa, craving isn't a bad thing. But the challenge is to realize God created us to crave so we'd ultimately desire more of Him in our lives, not more food. Many of us have misplaced the craving for God with an overindulgence in physical pleasures. In this six-session small group Bible study, you will come to understand how cravings for lasting spiritual satisfaction are often mistaken for cravings for food.

Unglued

The disruption of strong emotions can feel jarring. It can feel like you're coming unglued . . . but you can learn how to make your emotions work for you instead of against you. In this six-session video Bible study, learn how to process emotions and resolve conflicts in ways that lead to wisdom, composure, and a more peaceful life.

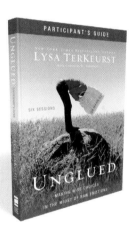

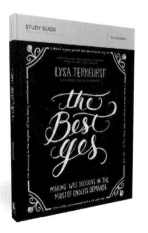

The Best Yes

There is a big difference between saying yes to everyone and saying yes to God. Learn four usable strategies for making wise decisions day by day that honor God in managing your time, reducing stress, doing your best for you family, and finding time for yourself. The power of "the best yes" is the choice that shapes all your other choices.

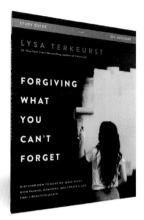

Forgiving What You Can't Forget

If you've ever felt stuck in a cycle of unresolved pain, playing offenses over and over in your mind—if you've ever been hurt so badly that you don't know if you'll ever get past it—discover what the Bible really says about forgiveness and how to find the peace that comes from embracing it. This six-session study will walk with you on a step-by-step process toward the grace of forgiveness and the freedom from the pain of past wrongs.

It's Not Supposed to Be This Way

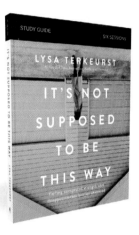

In this six-session video Bible study, *New York Times* bestselling author Lysa TerKeurst offers a safe place to share your disappointments, fresh biblical insights to get you through painful situations, and life-giving perspectives for living between Eden and eternity. Our disappointments can be the divine appointments our souls need to radically encounter God.

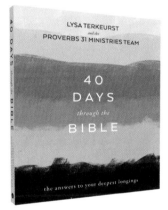

40 Days Through the Bible

In this personal Bible study, you will take a journey through the storyline of the Bible in 40 days so you can see major themes, how they are all connected and what that means for us as we read the Bible today. Discover the eight major things humanity longs for and how Jesus fulfills all of them for us, and stop the endless cycle of seeking and searching for satisfaction and find the answers to your deepest longings.

Good Boundaries and Goodbyes

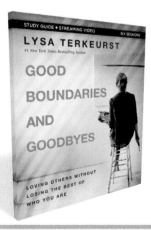

This six-session video Bible study with Lysa will equip you to determine the amount of access someone has to you, to stop being misled by weaponized Scriptures, to overcome ineffective boundary-setting with biblical principles and be equipped to say goodbye using three types of goodbyes found in God's Word.